PUB WALKS ALONG
The Tarka Trail

TWENTY CIRCl

GW00326257

Michael Bennie

COUNTRYSIDE BOOKS
NEWBURY, BERKSHIRE

COUNTRYSIDE BOOKS
3 Catherine Road
Newbury, Berkshire

To view our complete range of books,
please visit us at
www.countrysidebooks.co.uk

ISBN 1 85306 616 8

Designed by Graham Whiteman
Cover illustration by Colin Doggett
Photographs and maps by the author

Produced through MRM Associates Ltd., Reading
Typeset by Techniset Typesetters, Newton-le-Willows, Merseyside
Printed by Woolnough Bookbinding Ltd., Irthlingborough

Contents

AREA MAP SHOWING LOCATION OF THE WALKS
TARKA TRAIL – SOUTHERN LOOP (WALKS 1–12)

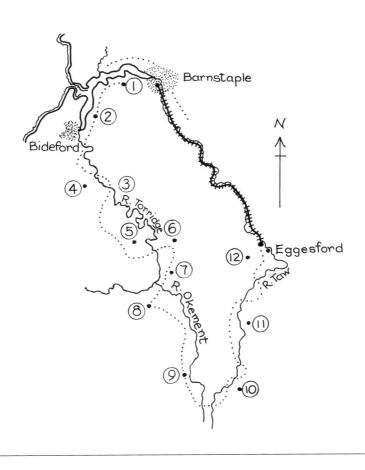

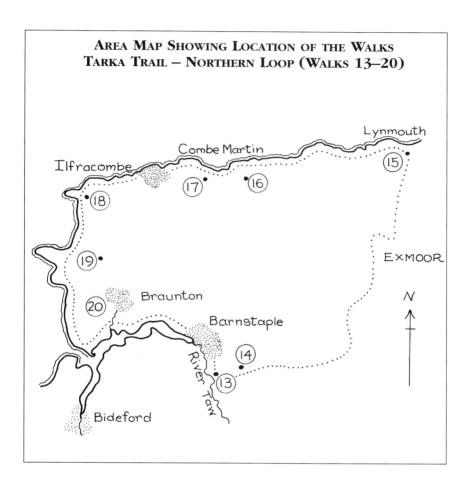

AREA MAP SHOWING LOCATION OF THE WALKS
TARKA TRAIL – NORTHERN LOOP (WALKS 13–20)

Lynmouth

Combe Martin

Ilfracombe

(15)

(17)   (16)

(18)

EXMOOR

(19)

N

Braunton

(20)

Barnstaple

(14)

River Taw

(13)

Bideford

Part Two: The Northern Loop

Walk

PUBLISHER'S NOTE

We hope that you obtain considerable enjoyment from this book; great care has been taken in its preparation. However, changes of landlord and actual closures are sadly not uncommon. Likewise, although at the time of publication all routes followed public rights of way or permitted paths, diversion orders can be made and permissions withdrawn.

We cannot of course be held responsible for such diversion orders and any inaccuracies in the text which result from these or any other changes to the routes nor any damage which might result from walkers trespassing on private property. We are anxious though that all details covering the walks and the pubs are kept up to date and would therefore welcome information from readers which would be relevant to future editions.

INTRODUCTION

Henry Williamson's classic book *Tarka the Otter* provides a superb evocation of the glorious North Devon countryside as it describes Tarka's adventures and follows his travels through 'the Country of the Two Rivers'.

Those rivers, the Taw and the Torridge, together with their tributaries, form the 'skeleton' for the Tarka Trail, a long-distance route which takes in most of the locations mentioned in the book. It stretches from Dartmoor's fringes to the Bristol Channel and covers some of the most beautiful landscapes to be seen in England: the rich, rolling North Devon farmland, the wide spaces of Exmoor, the awesome cliffs, quiet coves and long sandy beaches along the coast and the deep green woods of the river valleys. It is some 180 miles long (about 20 miles of which comprises a train journey along the Tarka Line and is inaccessible on foot) and takes the form of a figure of eight centred on Barnstaple. The southern section takes in the two rivers themselves and their tributaries, while the northern loop explores the scenes of Tarka's exploits on Exmoor and along the coast.

The Trail is part of the Tarka Project, which was initiated in 1988 by Devon County Council and the various district councils in the area, with the aim of enriching the surrounding wildlife and beauty and encouraging public enjoyment. The conservation aspects of the Project's work are now overseen by a charitable trust, the Tarka Country Trust; if you would like more information on its work, or on the Trail generally, you will find the Tarka Project office very helpful. It is based at Bideford Railway Station, East-the-Water, Bideford.

This collection comprises 20 circular walks, each of which takes in a section of the Trail, and each of which starts and finishes at a convenient hostelry. Most of the pubs almost select themselves: warm, welcoming establishments oozing character and with menus to match. Others, chosen perhaps for their locations rather than their character, may not have any special features to make them stand out but are nevertheless pleasant, congenial places to stop for refreshment. But they are almost as varied as the areas they serve, ranging from a 17th century folly to a Victorian railway station, and from a 12th century dower house to a 1920s hotel. The pub entries are intended to convey just a flavour of the place, but I have tried to give all the information you might need to enjoy your visit, including suggestions about where to park.

There are detailed descriptions of the routes of the walks and sketch maps to help you orientate yourselves. The Tarka Trail itself is for the most part well signposted, although on those stretches which follow the South West Coast Path or the Two Moors Way it may be the signs or waymarks of those two routes that are shown. The walks vary a great deal in difficulty; some are easy ambles along almost flat, mostly surfaced tracks, while others, especially those that follow the coastline, involve a lot of climbing. The brief introductions to the walks usually indicate what you can expect in this regard, Note, too, that although the Tarka Trail itself is generally well maintained, some of the paths and tracks leading to it may become overgrown or muddy at times. I have tried to indicate where this is likely to present problems, but as a general rule I would suggest that long trousers and substantial shoes or boots should be worn wherever the route follows farm paths or tracks.

For those who like to have more detail, the relevant Ordnance Survey map is recommended and I have noted the appropriate Ordnance Survey sheets for each walk. The Landranger maps cover a larger area than the Outdoor Leisure or the new Explorer series, but the scale is smaller (1:50 000 as opposed to 1:25 000) and they are consequently less detailed. There are also 'link' sections at the beginning or end of each route description where applicable, giving a brief outline of those segments of the Tarka Trail not included in the book, for those who want to combine two walks or who want to cover the whole Trail.

This is a delightfully varied and often breathtakingly beautiful route; I hope you enjoy exploring it as much as I have.

Michael Bennie

WALK 1

FREMINGTON
The New Inn

This is the scene of the 'Great Winter' so graphically described in 'Tarka the Otter'. It is also where Tarka and his mate caught a wild swan.

The Tarka Trail starts at a gentle pace, following a disused railway line alongside the River Taw. We join it near the village of Fremington and follow it for over 3 miles to Instow. It is a fascinating stretch with varied wildlife – marshes on one side and farm fields on the other. At Instow the route turns inland and follows quiet, hedge-fringed lanes before cutting across through a lovely wood to return to Fremington. It is mainly very easy walking, with just one fairly short climb after leaving Instow.

The New Inn is an attractive old pub with a very welcoming atmosphere. It is fairly long and narrow, with a small, snug little bar on the left near the main door, a larger, airy lounge further down the passage, an attractive dining room on the right and a pretty little courtyard at the back.

9

The lounge is beautifully decorated with an interesting collection of knick-knacks, and there are some delightful pictures and epigrams painted on the walls, including the following: 'What a caterpillar calls the end of the world, the Master calls a butterfly.' Both dogs and children are allowed, and accommodation is available. The inn is open from 11 am to 3 pm and 5.30 pm to 11 pm on weekdays, with the usual restricted Sunday hours.

A wide range of tipples is offered on draught: Courage Directors, John Smith's, Wadworth 6X and Triple Crown bitters, Miller's Pilsner, Foster's and Kronenbourg lagers, Guinness, Caffrey's ale and Woodpecker and Inch's Stonehouse cider. If you are looking for more solid sustenance, there is a wide-ranging menu, from sandwiches to steaks and roasts. The pub is particularly proud of its salmon roulade. Telephone: 01271 373859.

- **GETTING THERE:** The pub is right on the B3233 towards the east of Fremington. The village is signposted from the A39 Barnstaple to Bideford road at the Roundswell roundabout, or it can be approached via Instow to the west.
- **PARKING:** The pub has a fairly large car park, and there is no objection to customers leaving their cars there while they walk. As a matter of courtesy, however, it would be a good idea to ask first.
- **LENGTH OF THE WALK:** 6¼ miles. Maps: OS Landranger 180 Barnstaple and Ilfracombe; OS Explorer 139 Bideford, Ilfracombe and Barnstaple (GR 513324).

THE TARKA TRAIL FROM BARNSTAPLE TO FREMINGTON PILL (3 MILES)

The Trail starts at Barnstaple Station. Turn left as you come out of the station and follow the signs under the bridge to join it on the disused stretch of railway line. After 3 miles you will come to a bridge over Fremington Pill; Walk 1 joins the Trail at this point.

THE WALK

1. Almost immediately across the main road from the pub, just slightly to the left, you will see a public footpath leading away between a wall on the left and a fence on the right. Follow it as it curves to the left through a gateway and then right again, in amongst some trees, with a wealth of flowers on either side, especially in spring. You come out at Fremington Pill ('pill' is a local word for a creek), and follow it down to

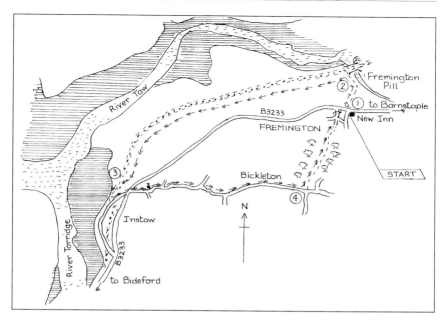

the River Taw, with a mass of rhododendrons on the left. Go through a gateway and down to a disused railway; this is the Tarka Trail and the South West Coast Path.

2. Turn left, and follow the Trail westward, initially between high hedges. Soon the trees thin out and you get a good view across the River Taw on your right, with farmland on your left. The Trail is as straight as a die for some 2 miles, but it is by no means without interest. There can be wild flowers in abundance, birds singing in the trees alongside and a variety of activity along the river. You also pass the rather weird-looking Isley Marsh Nature Reserve, with its strange mounds and channels. At the end of Isley Marsh, the Coast Path takes a detour to the right to follow the estuary more closely, but the Tarka Trail stays on the disused railway line.

After 2 miles of dead-straight walking, the Trail curves to the left a little, and you come to a gate. Go round it, cross a track and go round the next gate. The next short stretch is not very prepossessing, as you pass a business park followed by an electricity substation, but you are soon among the more attractive riverside scenery again, with the dunes of Braunton Burrows Nature Reserve across the river on your right and the houses of Appledore climbing the hill ahead. You pass a few cottages and cross a track, and soon you will see an old railway bridge crossing the track ahead. Shortly before you reach it, leave the Tarka Trail via a path on your right leading to a car park; turn left and at the road turn left again.

3. Cross the old railway bridge, and after about 250 yards you will come to the B3233. Cross it and follow the lane on the other side (signposted to Bickleton). You pass the lovely old Barton farmhouse on your right, and at the junction follow the main lane past the parish church. It twists and climbs between banks filled with an array of flowers. At the next junction, by the school, follow the main lane straight on (again signposted to Bickleton). It continues to climb, but rather more gently now, and at the top you get a lovely view over the river to your left.

After about 1/2 mile, you come to another junction; follow the main lane again (still signposted to Bickleton), and again at the next. The lane begins to descend, and you get another marvellous view across the river on your left. After 700 yards you pass through the hamlet of Bickleton, and 500 yards beyond that you will come to a lane going sharp right, with a public footpath sign pointing left into a wood.

4. Turn left here and follow the track through the trees. This is a lovely stretch of woodland, with a stream over on your right and flowers all around, and you are accompanied throughout by birdsong. The track can be a bit muddy at times, but it is not difficult to pick your way around any problematic patches.

After about 1/2 mile you pass a small weir on the stream and emerge from the wood into a field. Keep to the right, following the white-topped posts. A kissing gate at the end of the field brings you out onto a track which leads you between some houses to a made-up road. Follow that to a more major road, and go straight on down that road to a T-junction at the B3233. Turn right and after a little over 100 yards you will find yourself back at the New Inn.

WALK 2

WESTLEIGH
The Westleigh Inn

❦

This section of the Trail follows the disused railway line alongside the lower reaches of the River Torridge. It is a beautiful, easy stroll and the outward walk to the attractive village of Instow (where Tarka almost had hot ashes thrown over him) is equally delightful, with some excellent views and a pretty stretch along farm paths and tracks.

This is a charming, unspoilt 15th century inn, full of character, tucked away off the beaten track, and visitors are made welcome by staff and locals alike. It comprises two cosy bars, one for non-smokers, a large beer garden with good views over the estuary of the Taw and the Torridge, and a children's play area.

There is a good selection of beers on tap – Bass, John Smith's, Ushers Best and Ruddles County are the regulars, and there is always one guest beer. In addition, you will find draught Blackthorn cider, Stella Artois, Kronenbourg and Foster's lagers, and Guinness. The food is mouthwatering in its variety, ranging from jacket potatoes to steaks. The home-made steak and Guinness pie is particularly good.

The inn is open from 11.30 am to 3 pm and 6 pm to 11 pm on weekdays and from 12 o'clock right through to 10.30 pm on Sundays, and both children and dogs are welcome. Telephone: 01271 860867.

● **GETTING THERE:** Follow the B3233, which runs north from the A39 at Bideford along the east bank of the River Torridge. Westleigh is signposted to the right after about $^3/_4$ mile. In the village, take the lane which leads off to the left and you will see the Westleigh Inn signposted to the left again.

● **PARKING:** There is a large pub car park, and there is no problem with parking there while walking (but please ask first). There is limited parking elsewhere in the village.

● **LENGTH OF THE WALK:** $4^1/_4$ miles. Maps: OS Landranger 180 Barnstaple and Ilfracombe; OS Explorer 139 Bideford, Ilfracombe and Barnstaple (GR 471287).

THE WALK

1. Turn left and make your way down to the lane through the village; turn left again and climb out into open country. At the top of the hill the lane twists and turns somewhat and you get the occasional view over rolling farms and woods to the right and across the estuary and out to sea to the left. At the junction go straight on (signposted to Treyhill and Barnacott), still with a lovely view to the right.

2. After another $^1/_2$ mile, you will see a public footpath sign on the right, pointing left up a track. Turn off the road here and follow the track round to the right. Shortly before you get to the farmhouse, you will see a rough track going left through a gate marked 'Heather's Way'. Go down there to another gate. Keep to the right of the field on the other side, and soon after the hedge curves to the right, bear left across the field to a small footbridge.

Go straight across the next field to a gate and across the farmyard beyond to a track. You will see a gate leading into a field on your left; go through that, rather than following the track straight on. Cross the field to a stile and then go diagonally left across the next field; you now get a very good view across Appledore and the estuary to the sea. You will come to a gate in the hedge on your right; go through it and bear left to another gate in the far corner of the next field. Go straight across the next field to a stile and up some steps into a lane. Turn right.

GREAT TORRINGTON
The Puffing Billy

This pretty route combines a wander across the bracken- and tree-covered expanse of Torrington Commons with a stroll through the attractive village of Weare Giffard and a delightful woodland amble. There is a bit of climbing on the Commons, but the paths are clear and the going fairly easy. The rest of the route follows a lane and the disused railway line between Bideford and Great Torrington, which forms the Tarka Trail at this point.

When the railway line between Torrington and Bideford was closed in 1982, Torrington Station was turned into a pub, and what else would it be called but the Puffing Billy? It still retains much of the appearance of a Victorian railway station, with the original platform now a beer garden and children's play area. Inside there is a large lounge overlooking the old railway track and a pleasant restaurant at the rear.

Children are made welcome, and they will be delighted by the animals and chickens in an enclosure off the beer garden. Indeed, it is very much a family-oriented pub, selling ice creams, soft drinks and sweets as well as coffee and cream teas and the usual pub fare. The food is of the traditional variety, ranging from sandwiches to steaks and home-made steak and kidney pie, and there are always a number of real ales on tap – the brews on offer change at regular intervals, so it is a case of turning up and taking pot luck. Other draught offerings include Kilkenny ale, Guinness, Tetley bitter and Lowenbrau and Carlsberg lagers.

Opening hours are to a certain extent at the discretion of the licensee. The pub opens all day on Sundays and during the school holidays, but at other times it may close during the afternoon if there are no customers. Dogs are allowed, but must be kept on the lead, even in the garden, because of the animals. Telephone: 01805 623050.

- **GETTING THERE:** Great Torrington is on the A386 between Bideford and Okehampton. The Puffing Billy is set back off the main road just outside the town on the Bideford side, and both it and the Tarka Trail, which runs alongside it, are well signposted from the road.
- **PARKING:** There is public parking in front of the pub and alongside.
- **LENGTH OF THE WALK:** $4^1/_2$ miles. Maps: OS Landranger 180 Barnstaple and Ilfracombe; OS Explorer 126 Clovelly and Hartland or 139 Bideford, Ilfracombe and Barnstaple (GR 479198).

THE WALK

1. Return to the main road and turn left to cross the bridge over the Tarka Trail. On the other side, just beyond a private drive, you will find a path going off to the left. Follow it into a wooded area. You are now on Torrington Commons. At the fork, go left and at the junction go left again. The path turns sharply to the right and you will see a stone alongside it, indicating that it is called Centenary Path. Cross over a footbridge and go straight on along the path on the other side (marked by another stone as Barmaid's Path). You soon leave the wood and climb gently up the side of a hill, surrounded by bracken and wild flowers.

At the fork, go left and after a short distance, turn left again onto a broad track. Follow this past a golf course, with a lovely view across the valley of the Torridge beyond it. At the end of the golf course, you emerge onto a broad lane.

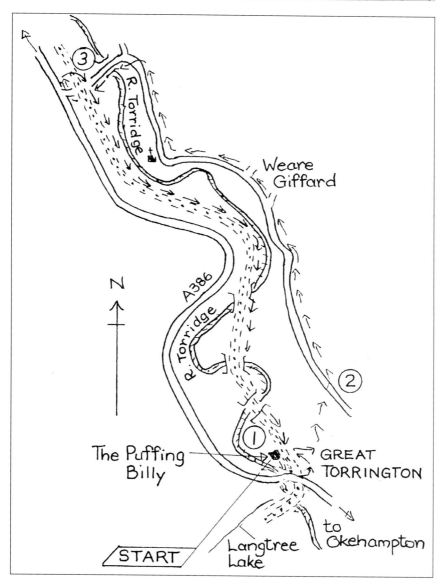

2. Turn left and follow the lane between high banks and hedges for about ³/₄ mile to Weare Giffard. The village is strung out along this lane in several segments, with open farmland in between, and comprises modern houses and traditional cottages.

You pass the village park on your left, and a bit later, after more open farmland, the lane turns sharp right and you will see Weare Giffard Hall, a very attractive 15th century manor house, and then the church, both on your left. After more farmland you will pass a few more houses. At the road junction, follow the main lane round to the left (signposted to Bideford and Monkleigh). It crosses the River Torridge via Halfpenny Bridge, which was built in the last century and derives its name from the halfpenny toll which those using it had to pay. It then passes the remains of Annery Kiln, an old lime kiln, before going under a railway bridge to join the A386. Just before the junction, turn right through a gap in a fence to join the Tarka Trail.

3. Turn right. Along this stretch, the Trail is fringed with trees which often meet overhead, forming a delightful green tunnel. From time to time there is an opening on the left, giving you a very good view across the river to Weare Giffard. You can occasionally hear the traffic on the main road on your right, but it is masked by trees on that side. The trees along here are mainly sycamore, elder and hazel, and alongside the track is a wide variety of flowers, including herb Robert, hogweed, buttercups, dog roses and cow parsley in summer.

You will cross two tracks which pass under the Trail; about 600 yards after the second, the Trail crosses the river, which twists and turns in a series of loops, 'like a serpent' as Williamson describes it. Look to your right here for a good view upriver to the impressive Canal Bridge, where he got his first inspiration for the book. Now a private driveway, as its name suggests it once carried a canal across the river. After about 300 yards you pass under a viaduct and cross another loop in the river, with a weir on the right, and 300 yards beyond that you cross yet again. After a further 500 yards or so you will find yourself back at the Puffing Billy. There is no access direct from the Trail, so you will have to go past the pub, through a gate and then round to the right to get to it.

THE TARKA TRAIL FROM THE PUFFING BILLY TO LANGTREE LAKE (1/2 MILE)

The Trail continues along the disused railway line, under the main road, and crosses the river again to reach the stream called Langtree Lake. A couple of hundred yards along the bank of the stream, it meets the route of the next walk.

WALK 4
FRITHELSTOCK
The Clinton Arms

*T*he *Tarka Trail continues to follow the disused railway line along this stretch, hugging the bank of the lovely Langtree Lake, which Tarka and his family followed to reach Merton Moors, through a beautiful wood. The route to the Trail passes the ruins of an old Augustinian priory, following a road and then a woodland track, with an extensive view across the North Devon countryside. The way back runs across fields, again with good views.*

The Clinton Arms is a relatively new pub; the old establishment burnt down in 1945. It does not give the impression of being modern, however – it has the appearance and character of a much older inn.

It comprises a pleasantly furnished bar, a snug lounge with deep armchairs, a restaurant and a lovely walled beer garden. There is also accommodation available for those who want a bit of a break, and a fly-fishing school behind the pub with a mile of fishing rights on the River Torridge for keen anglers.

21

Both children and dogs are welcome, and the weekday opening hours are 12 noon to 3 pm and 5.30 pm to 11 pm. On Sunday evenings the pub opens at 7 pm and closes at 10.30 pm. Bass and Tetley bitter are the regular draught ales, with a guest beer which changes from time to time. Also on tap are Carlsberg lager and Carlsberg Export, Blackthorn cider and Guinness. Food is available both at midday and in the evening, and ranges from sandwiches and salads to delicious home-made steak and kidney and cottage pies and the chef's pasta specialities. Telephone: 01805 623279.

● **GETTING THERE:** Turn west off the A386 Great Torrington to Bideford road just north of Great Torrington and follow the signs to Frithelstock.

● **PARKING:** The pub has a car park at the side, and there is no objection to customers leaving their cars there while they walk. There is also a certain amount of parking around the village green at the front.

● **LENGTH OF THE WALK:** 4 miles. Maps: OS Landranger 180 Barnstaple and Ilfracombe; OS Explorer 126 Clovelly and Hartland (GR 464195). (Note: the Explorer map has the village name as Frithstock, but the Landranger map and the village sign use Frithelstock.)

THE WALK

1. Immediately across the road from the pub is the church and the remains of Frithelstock Priory, a 15th century Augustinian establishment. It is on private property, but you can see it over the wall of the churchyard to the right of the church.

To continue the walk, turn east along the road through the village (right from the pub, left from the church). It takes you out of the village and you get a very good view ahead over the Torridge valley, before it begins to descend into the valley itself.

2. After about 3/4 mile you will see a road going off to the left. Immediately opposite it is a track; turn right here and follow the track alongside a wood, with a high hedge on your right. It bends to the right, leading you into a wood, and you will begin to hear Langtree Lake bubbling along on your left ('lake' in this part of the world refers to a stream, not a large expanse of water).

The track leads to a house; just before you reach it, turn sharp left down a path to a gate. Cross the field beyond to a footbridge over Langtree Lake followed by another gate, which brings you out onto the disused railway line and the Tarka Trail.

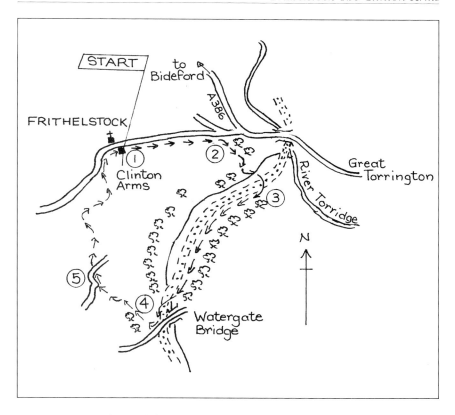

3. Turn right and follow the Trail through a stretch of woodland alongside Langtree Lake. This is an idyllic part of the route: the walking is easy, the wood is full of birdsong, the track is flanked by a magnificent display of wild flowers according to the season and you are never far from the meandering stream on your right.

After about $1^1/_2$ miles the track crosses the stream. You continue for about 200 yards on the other side before emerging through a gate onto a road at Watergate Bridge.

4. Turn right along the road and after about 50 yards, just beyond a track, look out for a public footpath sign on the right; it is not very easy to see, as it is hidden by trees, and the path it is indicating can become a little overgrown. Turn right off the road and follow the path into a wood; it becomes clearer as you go. It leads to a gate which takes you into a field.

Go diagonally left up the field, a little way away from the wood on your left, to a gap in the hedge. Cross the next field to a gate and keep to the left of the next one to another gate leading onto a track. Turn left and follow the track round to the right past some farm buildings. It comes out at a lane; turn right.

5. After about 150 yards, as the lane bends to the right, go left through a gate, following the public footpath sign. Follow the track along the edge of the field, and when it turns to the left, carry on round to the right along the edge of the field, following the direction of another footpath sign.

At the end of the field you come to another track; turn left, again following the footpath sign, and follow the track round to the right to a gate. Carry on straight up the field beyond, and when the track peters out, go straight on to meet a hedge on your left. Keep to the right of the hedge and at the end of the field follow it round to the right. As you go, you get another good view over the rolling fields and woods to your right.

About 300 yards after turning the corner of the field, look out for a gap in the hedge on your left with a stile. This leads into another field; cross it, aiming to the left of the house you can see ahead. As you come over the brow of the hill, you will see a house on your left with a gate to the right of it. Go down to the gate and out into the road beyond; turn right to return to Frithelstock and the Clinton Arms.

THE TARKA TRAIL FROM WATERGATE BRIDGE TO DUNSBEAR MOOR (4¹/₄ MILES)

There is a car park across the road at Watergate Bridge, and then the disused railway continues alongside Langtree Lake. The Trail follows it through the clay country above the Torridge until the next walk joins it at a road crossing at Dunsbear Moor.

WALK 5
MERTON
The Malt Scoop Inn
❧❀❧

The main attraction of this route is the abundance of flora you will see along the way. The lanes are filled with flowers for most of the spring and summer, and this stretch of the Tarka Trail passes through some lovely woodland. There are also the claypits, now largely obscured by trees, where Tarka and his family played with Marland Jimmy. We take quiet lanes and farm paths to the Trail, which still follows the disused railway here, and then there is easy road walking back to Merton.

The Malt Scoop is an interesting old coaching inn dating from the 16th and 17th centuries, which has been in the same family since 1906. There are two parts to it: two delightfully furnished little snug rooms and a slightly bigger cellar room – beautifully cool in summer – at one end, and the large Stable Bar at the other, separated by the private accommodation. They are never used at the same time: the bar is only open in the evenings and at weekends, while the three smaller rooms are used at midday during the week.

The pub is open from 12 noon to 2 pm and 7 pm to 11 pm on Mondays to Saturdays, with the usual restricted Sunday hours. Both children and dogs are very welcome. The cask-conditioned ale is Bishop's Finger, and Ansells and Tetley bitters are also served, alongside Carlsberg and Carlsberg Export lagers, Old Rascal cider and Guinness on tap. These are only available in the Stable Bar, so if you order a beer at lunchtime during the week, the landlord has to go all the way round to fetch it! Food is restricted to bar snacks – pasties and sandwiches – but they are delicious. Telephone: 01805 603260.

Before you leave Merton, you may also like to explore Barometer World, a fascinating museum of barometers which is just up the road from the pub.

- **GETTING THERE:** Merton is on the A386 between Okehampton and Great Torrington, and the Malt Scoop is in the centre of the village, right on the main road.
- **PARKING:** The pub car park is on the opposite side of the road, and there is no objection to customers leaving their cars there while they walk. Alternatively, there is a large free car park in front of the church to the south of the village.
- **LENGTH OF THE WALK:** 5 miles. Maps: OS Landranger 180 Barnstaple and Ilfracombe (start and finish) and 191 Okehampton and North Dartmoor (middle section); OS Explorer 127 South Molton and Chulmleigh (GR 527122).

THE WALK

1. Turn right onto the A386 and follow it through the village for 50 yards or so until you see Grange Lane on your right. Turn right here and then immediately right again into Limers' Lane. This takes you past some houses and out of the village between high, frequently flower-filled banks and hedges.

At the top of the hill it turns sharply to the left; follow it round, and as you do so, you get a good view over the hedges ahead of you. The lane begins to descend. At the bottom it crosses a small stream and turns sharply to the right.

2. Here you have a choice. If you prefer farm paths to roads, you can turn off left across a stile, following the direction of the public footpath sign. Cross the field on the other side to a hedge. When you reach it, go to the right of it; there is a clearly visible path between it and the crops to your right.

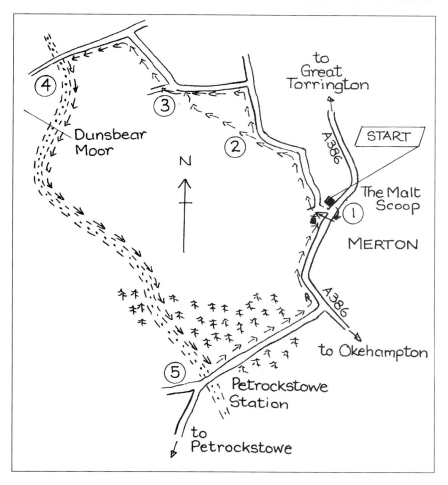

Go through the gap in the hedge at the end into the next field, and keep to the left of that, alongside the hedge again. Go through the next hedge and turn right to follow it alongside the next field. At the end, follow it round to the left and look out for a stile on your right about halfway along the field. Cross the stile into a lane and turn left.

If you prefer to use the lane, then follow it round to the right and climb the short hill out of the valley. After 500 yards, you will come to a junction; turn left. About 600 yards further on, the path across the fields joins the lane.

3. At the next junction, follow the main lane round to the right to descend into another valley. The banks and hedges along here are ablaze with colour in the summer, with foxgloves, buttercups, red campion, hedge woundwort, nipplewort, hogweed and many other flowers vying to outdo each other. The lane dips down into a valley and climbs up the other side, passing a farm as it does so.

At the T-junction turn left and follow this new lane past another farm and down a short hill until it crosses the disused railway, with the Tarka Trail waymark on the gates leading onto it on either side. There is also a signpost, but it is somewhat obscured by trees.

4. Turn left to join the Trail. Initially there are fields on your left and a wood on your right, but soon the trees close in on both sides. It is very pretty along here with an arch of trees overhead and a wealth of flowers alongside the track. It is also beautifully peaceful, the silence only broken by the song of the birds and the occasional bleating of a sheep in the fields beyond the trees.

After about $3/_4$ mile, you come to a road leading to a quarry; cross it. You will now occasionally hear the sounds of the quarrying on your left for another mile. Then the Trail enters a plantation. After a while the trees open up on the right and you get a pleasant view over the woods and farmland.

5. You finally come to a gate leading onto a road; go through and turn left. Follow the road through the plantation for about $3/_4$ mile to its junction with the A386. Turn left and follow this road for about $1/_2$ mile. Although it is a fairly major road, there is a pavement the whole way back to Merton.

THE TARKA TRAIL FROM PETROCKSTOWE STATION TO NEW BRIDGE ($3^1/_2$ MILES)

The Trail continues from the old Petrockstowe Station, now a car park. It then follows the disused railway line for about $1^1/_4$ miles before leaving it via a stile on the left and following farm paths to the A386. Turn left and walk alongside the road to Broadmead Cross, then turn right. From here the Trail follows the road north-east to cross the River Torridge at New Bridge. The next walk joins it just a couple of hundred yards beyond the bridge.

DOLTON
The Royal Oak

*This is a walk for those who enjoy the delights of quiet country lanes –
colourful displays of hedgerow flowers in season, sudden views of rolling
green farmland and a silence broken only by the song of the birds
mingling with the breeze-softened bleating of the sheep in the fields
around. It follows two segments of the Tarka Trail: first the stretch south
from Dolton along farm paths, and then the approach to the village,
mainly along tracks and lanes. The two are connected by more lanes to
make an easy circular route.*

For its size, Dolton is remarkably well supplied with pubs; there are
three, and they all have a great deal to commend them. But the Royal
Oak is my choice, partly because of its situation – the Tarka Trail goes
right past the front door – but mainly because of its character and
atmosphere, and the warm welcome visitors receive.

It is a very old building; the snug was the village well house – the well is now covered by a concrete slab – and has been dated to the 14th century, while the rest of the building is 16th century. Apart from the snug, there is an attractive, intimate bar and a delightful restaurant at the front, with a family games room at the back, all decorated with dried flowers strung along the beams and mantelpieces. There is also a small garden and a children's play area at the back, as well as tables in The Square at the front, where you can watch the village go about its business as you enjoy your refreshments.

Dogs are allowed, as long as they are on leads, and children are welcomed – indeed, this is a very family-friendly pub. The food is wide-ranging, with something to suit all tastes, from filled baguettes to steaks, and includes a children's menu. Particularly popular are 'sizzlers' – oriental rice served on a skillet, with a range of toppings, including such delights as Cajun chicken. You will also find a variety of drinks on draught: Flowers, Tetley and a range of guest beers, plus Whitbread Trophy, Labatt's, Stella Artois, Carlsberg and Carlsberg Export lagers, Thatcher's cider and Guinness.

The Royal Oak is open from 11 am to 2.30 pm and 6 pm to 11 pm on Mondays to Saturdays, with the usual more restricted Sunday hours. Accommodation is available for those who want to explore this lovely area more thoroughly. Telephone: 01805 804288.

- **GETTING THERE:** The village is on the B3217, which runs between Okehampton and Barnstaple. It can also be approached from the A386 Okehampton to Torrington road, from which it is signposted. The Royal Oak is set back in the old centre of the village. If you are approaching from the south, turn left just past the church, up Church Street; if you are coming from the north, turn right beyond the Union Inn, along Fore Street. Both will bring you out at The Square, one side of which is taken up by the pub.
- **PARKING:** There is parking outside in The Square and in the road, and a few spaces at the back of the pub.
- **LENGTH OF THE WALK:** $4^{1}/_{2}$ miles. Maps: OS Landranger 191 Okehampton and North Dartmoor; OS Explorer 127 South Molton and Chulmleigh (GR 569121).

THE WALK
Note: Because Dolton lies in the middle of the stretch of the Tarka Trail followed in this walk, the second half – the route out of Dalton – is described first. If you are walking the whole Trail, therefore, you will

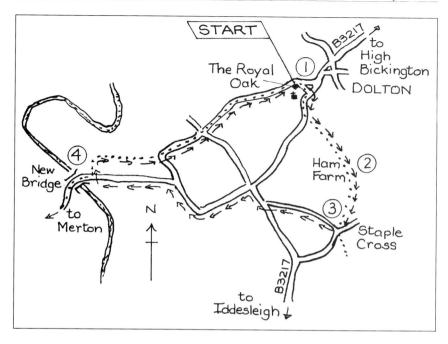

come to the part described towards the end of the route description – point 4, the approach to Dolton – first.

🐾 **1.** Turn right in The Square, and go down Church Street, past the post office and shop. At the T-junction by the church, turn right again. Follow the road out of the village and down a hill. Where it turns quite sharply to the right, go straight on through a gate. Cross the field beyond, and at the bottom cross a stile. Turn left across a wooden footbridge, and go up a short track on the other side into another field. Follow the hedge round to the right to another gate, and keep to the right of the next field to a third gate. This leads onto a track leading to a farm. Carry straight on and at the fork go right, following the sign to the farmhouse. Follow the track round to the right of the house.

2. Go through a gate and turn left along the edge of the field on the other side. At the bottom cross a stile, followed by a footbridge and another stile. Keep to the right of the hedge on the other side and follow it all the way up to the end of the field. At the top, you will find a gateway; go through and bear right to cross the next field to a stile. If you look back now, you will get a very good view across the lush green farmland. Cross the next field to a gate, and as you go you get another pleasant view over to the right.

3. The gate brings you to Staple Cross; this is where you leave the Tarka Trail temporarily. Turn sharp right (signposted to Dolton and Merton) and follow a lane between high hedges, with another good view ahead of you. There is an abundance of wild flowers along these lanes; depending on the season, you will find hedge bedstraw, meadowsweet, marsh thistle, bush vetch, buttercup, clover, red campion, nipplewort, foxglove, honeysuckle and many more.

After about ¹/₂ mile you will come to a T-junction; turn right along the B3217 (signposted to Dolton and Merton again). The views continue to enchant as you follow this road to a crossroads; turn left. After about 600 yards, this new lane bends sharply to the right; follow it round. After another 500 yards, there is a junction; follow the main lane round to the left (signposted to Torrington, Merton and Hatherleigh). About 700 yards further on, you will find a track leading off to the right, signposted 'Tarka Trail, public footpath'.

4. Turn up here to rejoin the Trail; where the track bends to the right, you will see a public footpath sign and the Tarka Trail waymark pointing right. Turn off here and go through a gate. Turn left along the edge of a field, and at the end follow the fence to the right. At the top of the field, cross a stile on the left and follow the path between a fence on your left and a bank on your right. Cross another stile, and the path broadens into a green lane lined with high banks of trees.

You emerge into a lane, and after about 500 yards come to a crossroads; carry straight on (signposted to Dolton). The lane begins to climb, but although it is quite a long ascent, it is fairly gentle. At the top you enter the village and the lane brings you out at The Square, with the Royal Oak on your right.

THE TARKA TRAIL FROM STAPLE CROSS TO EASTPARK (2¹/₄ MILES)

Take the track to Staple Farm. Go round the farm, then across some fields to a track. Follow the track to Upcott, go left at the road and then right up a lane. Go through a gate on the left and cross more fields. Bear right along another track and after some distance cross a road, continuing along the track on the other side to Eastpark.

IDDESLEIGH
The Duke of York
❦

Narrow lanes and farm paths are the main features of this walk. It follows the Trail out of the attractive thatched village of Iddesleigh and across the lush, rolling farmland that is seen throughout this part of Devon. The route back is along quiet lanes and more farm paths before another stretch of the Tarka Trail takes you into Iddesleigh again.

Iddesleigh is a very pretty little village, and the Duke of York is very much in keeping with its setting – a long, thatched 15th century building, originally a row of cottages built to house the workers on the village church. It is a delightful place to relax; there are no juke boxes or fruit machines, just old beams, inglenooks and a homely atmosphere. It comprises a large bar and a smaller restaurant, both with open fireplaces, and a secluded garden at the rear. There is also accommodation for those who are contemplating a longer stay. The pub is open all day, and both children and dogs are welcome.

The bar fare is extensive and varied, from salads to steaks, fish to vegetarian dishes, and there is a separate restaurant menu. For a snack that is almost a meal, try one of the 'chunky bandwiches', enormous sandwiches with a variety of fillings. There is an equally extensive range of drinks on offer. Cotleigh Tawney and Adnam's Broadside are usually on tap, plus a guest beer, and there is an interesting selection of ciders: Stowford Press, Thatcher's and Mendip Magic. Add to that four lagers – Stella Artois, Budweiser Budwar, Heineken and Red Stripe – plus Whitbread Trophy, Guinness and Guinness Bitter, and you have a range of draught beers and ciders to suit almost any taste. Telephone: 01837 810253.

- **GETTING THERE:** The village is on the B3217 between Dolton and Monkokehampton. The pub is set back slightly from the main road.
- **PARKING:** There is no pub car park, but there is parking around the green outside and along the roads in the village.
- **LENGTH OF THE WALK:** 4¼ miles. Maps: OS Landranger 191 Okehampton and North Dartmoor; OS Explorer 113 Okehampton (GR 569083).

THE WALK

Note: Because Iddesleigh is actually on the Tarka Trail, the second section of this part of the Trail – the route from Iddesleigh to Weekmore Cross – is described first. If you are walking the whole Trail, therefore, you will come to the segment described at the end of the route description – point 6, the short stretch from Eastpark to Iddesleigh – first.

1. Turn right as you leave the pub to return to the main road; turn right again. This is the route of the Tarka Trail. Where the road curves to the right, turn left down a lane (signposted to Week). When it bends to the left, follow it round, and about ½ mile after leaving the village you will come to a small stream, with a track on the right immediately beyond it.

2. Turn off here, as indicated by the Tarka Trail signpost, and follow the track among some trees to a gate. Carry straight on along the right-hand side of the field on the other side to another gate and keep to the right of the next field. You get a very pleasant view across the hedge to the right as you do so.

Go through another gate and round to the left of some farm

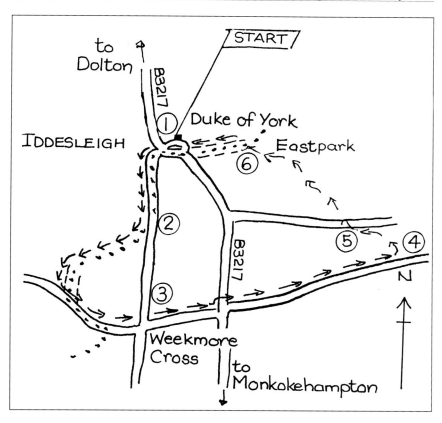

buildings to yet another one. Turn left along the track beyond, and at the lane at the end turn left again. After about 500 yards the Tarka Trail swings sharp right through a gateway; you should continue along the lane for a few more yards to Weekmore Cross.

3. Go straight across (signposted to Waldons). The lane runs dead straight for 600 yards until it meets a road (the B3217, although it is not marked as such on the signpost) at a T-junction. Turn left (signposted to Iddesleigh) and after a few yards right (signposted to Bullhead).

After about 700 yards you will see a public footpath sign pointing to the left. Ignore this and continue along the lane for a further ¹/₂ mile or so to another footpath, also on the left, immediately opposite the entrance to Bullhead Farm.

4. Turn off here through a gate. Keep to the right of the field beyond, and as you come over the brow of the hill, you get a very good view half left to Iddesleigh and beyond. Cross what remains of a stile at the end of the field and bear left across the next field to a gate leading into a lane; turn left. You pass a farm on the right and a pretty cottage on the left.

5. Immediately opposite the cottage is a gate leading into a green lane. There should be a public footpath sign pointing the way, but last time I was there it seemed to have disappeared. Go through the gate and follow the green lane; it can become overgrown and also muddy in places, so trousers and boots are recommended, but it is generally quite passable. (If you do have difficulties, or if you would rather not negotiate the nettles and mud, then you can simply continue along the lane and turn right at the T-junction to return to Iddesleigh.) The green lane leads you down alongside a wood on the right and crosses a stream. On the other side it goes to the left to a gate.

Keep to the hedge on the right-hand side of the field beyond and after 100 yards you will find a gate on your right; go through it and cross a little stream. Go up the next field, keeping to the hedge on the left and follow it round to the left to a gap in another hedge and then to a gateway at the end of the next field. This takes you onto a rough track across another field; follow it round to the left of some farm buildings and then to the right to a gate onto a much clearer track just by the buildings.

6. This is Eastpark, and this is where you rejoin the Tarka Trail. Turn left and follow the track back to Iddesleigh. Turn right in the village to return to the Duke of York.

HATHERLEIGH
The George Hotel
❧❀❧

This part of mid-Devon is an area of rich pastureland, picturesque farmhouses, rolling hills, flower-filled hedgerows, quietly meandering rivers and narrow lanes. You will be given a taste of all these and more on this undemanding route. The Tarka Trail winds along farm paths and tracks here, enabling you to enjoy the special beauty of the countryside, while the rest of the route is along quiet lanes, with some excellent views.

The George is a delightful old thatched coaching inn in the centre of this pretty little market town. Built round a cobbled courtyard, it is approached through arches at either end. The bar is towards the back, on the way to the car park, and is an attractive L-shaped room with bare stone walls and leaded windows, furnished with settles and tables. There is a family room off the main bar and tables out in the courtyard, and children and dogs are welcome in both, but not in the main bar. Accommodation is, of course, available too.

The food ranges from sandwiches, jacket potatoes and salads to mixed grills and a variety of fish, chicken, steak and vegetarian dishes. There are also special children's menus. The resident real ales are Bass, Dartmoor Best and Hicks, and there is one guest beer. Other draught offerings are Whitbread Best bitter, Castlemaine and Stella Artois lager, Stowford Press and Sam's Dry cider, Kilkenny ale and Guinness. The opening hours are from 11 am to 3 pm and 6 pm to 11 pm on Mondays to Saturdays and the usual more restricted Sunday hours. Telephone: 01837 810454.

- **GETTING THERE:** Hatherleigh is just off the A386 between Okehampton and Torrington, and is clearly signposted. The George Hotel is in the centre of the town.
- **PARKING:** There is a car park behind the hotel. Follow the signs to the public parking off Bridge Street, on the way into town, and bear right to reach the hotel car park. There is no objection to customers leaving their cars there while they walk.
- **LENGTH OF THE WALK:** 4³/₄ miles. Maps: OS Landranger 191 Okehampton and North Dartmoor; OS Explorer 113 Okehampton (GR 541045).

THE WALK

Note: Hatherleigh lies directly on the Tarka Trail, so the second section of this part of the Trail – the short stretch out of Hatherleigh – is described first. If you are walking the whole Trail, therefore, you will come to the last part – points 3 and 4 of the route description, from Weekmore Cross to Hatherleigh – first.

1. Leave the hotel by the front entrance, turn right and cross the road to High Street. This is the route of the Tarka Trail out of Hatherleigh. Follow it to a crossroads and bear left into Victoria Road.

The road climbs gently out of town. At the top of the rise you get a magnificent view to the right across to Dartmoor, and you will come to a Tarka Trail signpost pointing across the field on the right. You should carry on along the road, however, and because the hedge is fairly low along here, you will continue to enjoy the view to Dartmoor on the right. At the junction, go straight on (signposted to Monkokehampton and Winkleigh). You now get another excellent view up ahead and to the left to complement the one to the right.

2. At the next junction turn left (signposted to Week and Iddesleigh),

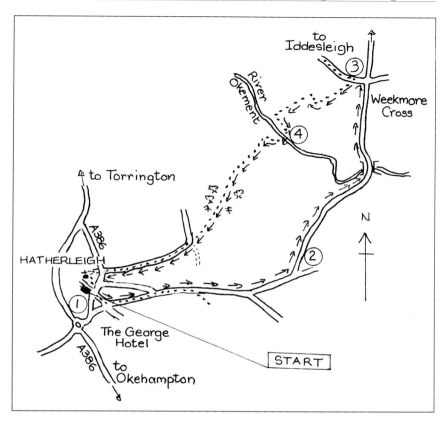

and a different view opens up ahead. The hedgerows alongside this lane are ablaze with colour in spring and summer. After about ¹/₂ mile, it swings to the right and then to the left, and begins to descend to the River Okement. It crosses the river via Iddesleigh Bridge and climbs gently up the valley on the other side. Just over ¹/₂ mile after crossing the river, you will come to Weekmore Cross. Turn left here (signposted to Nethercott and Bridge Town).

🐾 **3.** Where the lane bends to the right, go straight on along a track, following the direction of the Tarka Trail signpost. As you follow the track, you can enjoy the views of Dartmoor again, this time on your left. The track leads to Nethercott Barton; when you reach the farm, go right, following the direction of the Tarka Trail signpost. Keep to the left of a field to a gate and turn left onto a track. It is beautifully peaceful here among the trees.

You come out at a gate into a field; go half left to another gate and turn right to follow the bank along the edge of the next field. At the end of the field you will find the River Okement again; turn left and follow the riverbank for 200 yards or so to a footbridge.

4. Cross the river and turn left. Follow the clear path between banks to a field; keep to the left to a gate, and turn right. Follow the hedge to cross a stile and turn left. About two-thirds of the way up the field, you will find a gate and a stile on the left; cross the stile and bear right across the next field to another stile. Go straight across the orchard on the other side to yet another stile into a farmyard.

Turn left along a metalled track to join a drive leading to Groves Fishleigh. Go through the yard to a gate and bear left to cross a stile. Go straight across the field beyond to another stile and across the next field to enter a wood. Bear right through the wood. Go through a kissing gate and across a small footbridge into a conifer plantation. At the path junction go straight on to a gate into a large field. Keep to the right to a gate, followed immediately by another one. Cross the next field to a gate in the far corner, and turn left along a lane. Follow the lane for just over ¹/₂ mile to a T-junction on the outskirts of Hatherleigh. Cross the road to Church Lane, follow it to the churchyard and turn left to return to the town centre and the George Hotel.

🐾 THE TARKA TRAIL FROM HATHERLEIGH TO GOLDBURN CROSS (6³/₄ MILES)

After leaving Hatherleigh, the Trail branches half right off the road and crosses three fields to a gate on the right and then goes alongside a lane. After a few hundred yards, it joins the lane via a gate. It follows the lane for 1¹/₂ miles before turning right to Cadham.

A little over ¹/₂ mile along this lane, it takes a track on the left to Higher Cadham Farm, goes round the farm and crosses two fields to a footbridge across the River Okement. It then goes right alongside the river to join the A3072, where it goes right again to Jacobstowe. Just beyond the road junction at Jacobstowe, it turns left down a lane and follows it for 2 miles to Goldburn Cross.

WALK 9

OKEHAMPTON
The White Hart Hotel
❦

This segment of the Tarka Trail is mainly through the delightful Abbeyford Woods, an extensive tract of conifers just outside Okehampton. To reach it, you follow winding, hedge-fringed lanes and easy farm tracks. Not only is the route a floral delight, but the views, particularly to the south across the wastes of Dartmoor, are magnificent.

There are, of course, several pubs in Okehampton, but the White Hart takes a lot of beating. Not only is it ideally situated, in the centre of Okehampton and directly on the Tarka Trail, but it is a delightful place to stop for a meal or a drink. It is an attractive coaching inn whose origins are buried in the distant past. What is known is that it was recognised as Okehampton's premier inn when it was granted a licence in the 17th century, and it has had a number of famous customers over the centuries: William Pitt the Elder, who was MP for Okehampton in the 18th century, held his celebration dinners there, and Emperor Haile

Selassie of Ethiopia was a frequent visitor during his exile in the 1930s.

There are two low-beamed bars decorated with prints, one of which is a children's and non-smoking area, and dogs are welcome in both. There is also an attractively and comfortably furnished restaurant towards the rear of the hotel. Accommodation is, of course, available for those who want a longer stay.

The bars are open all day, from 10.30 am to 11 pm (11.30 am to 10.30 pm on Sundays), and offer a good range of beers and other drinks. Wadworth 6X and Speckled Hen are usually available, as well as Boddingtons and Tinners Ale, plus Worthington and Whitbread Best, Carlsberg, Heineken and Stella Artois lager and Murphy's stout. The food is equally varied, ranging from sandwiches and ploughman's lunches to the popular steak and kidney pudding and a selection of vegetarian dishes. You might like to try the cod done in the hotel's own batter – made with beer. Telephone: 01837 52730.

- **GETTING THERE:** The A30 Exeter to Cornwall road bypasses Okehampton to the south, and the town is clearly signposted from both directions. The A386 Bideford road passes to the west, and Okehampton is again clearly signposted. The White Hart is in Fore Street, the main street through the town.
- **PARKING:** The hotel car park is at the rear; turn south down George Street to reach it. There is no objection to patrons leaving cars there while they walk, but please tell the hotel receptionist that you are doing so. Alternatively, there is public parking off Market Street, which runs north opposite the hotel.
- **LENGTH OF THE WALK:** 5½ miles. Maps: OS Landranger 191 Okehampton and North Dartmoor; OS Explorer 113 Okehampton (GR 588951).

THE WALK

1. Turn right into Fore Street and follow it for about 300 yards until you see Northfield Road on your left. Turn into it and immediately right into Crediton Road, following the sign for cycle route 27. At the second crossroads bear left, following the signpost to North Tawton and Crediton and at the roundabout bear right (still signposted to North Tawton and Crediton). You now leave the bustle of the town centre behind you and follow a quiet suburban road (still called Crediton Road) as it climbs gently out of town.

2. Just beyond the derestriction sign, turn left down Chichacott Road. You pass a few houses on the left and then find yourself in open country, with high banks full of wild flowers on either side. The lane

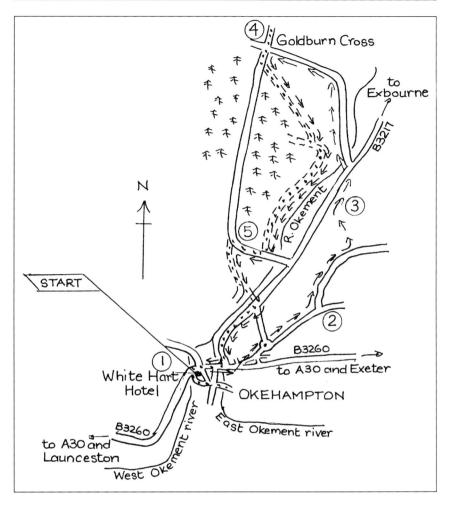

takes you down past a farm and swings to the left to cross a stream and climb steeply up the other side.

Near the top of the hill you will see a track on the left, with a public bridleway sign. Turn down it, and after a while you will get an excellent view over the hedge to the left across the outskirts of Okehampton to the stark tors of Dartmoor beyond. The track begins to descend steeply past a wood with pheasant pens alongside and ends at a gate. Go through and bear left along a narrower path which skirts a field, with a line of gorse on the right. It goes down among some trees and bears right across another field to a gate leading onto a drive, which in turn takes you to a road, the B3217.

3. Turn right and then, after 300 yards, turn left along a lane (signposted to Goldburn). It crosses the River Okement and turns sharply to the right to follow the line of the river downstream. Soon you will hear the river burbling on your right and then you will see it through the trees. This is a lovely stretch among the trees, with the river alternately splashing over rocks and murmuring through quiet pools at the bottom of a steep bank alongside you.

After a while the lane and the river diverge again and the lane bends sharply to the left to climb steadily out of the valley. As it does so you get another very good view across to Dartmoor. Just over ¹/₂ mile after leaving the river you come to Goldburn Cross.

4. Turn left, following the cycle signs; the actual signpost once indicated that this lane goes to Hook, but that reference has been painted out. This is where you join the Tarka Trail. The lane takes a slight bend to the left and then, as it curves slightly to the right again, you will see a Tarka Trail signpost pointing left down a track. Turn off here, go through a gateway and follow the broad track on the other side, with a lovely view across the farms and woods ahead.

The track curves along the edge of Abbeyford Woods, an extensive and delightful plantation with some smaller deciduous trees in amongst the conifers. You eventually come to a T-junction; turn left to follow a new track downhill. It twists and turns and from time to time you come to cleared areas; and when you do, you get more superb views across to the barren wastes of Dartmoor ahead of you.

5. After about 1¹/₂ miles of attractive woodland walking, you emerge onto a lane. Turn right and climb for about 300 yards until the lane turns sharp right; turn left here, down a track, following the Tarka Trail sign. After a while you will see Okehampton ahead of you, with Dartmoor beyond. The track leads down to a farm; go through the yard and out the other side along a lane. Where it turns right, go straight on along a path, following the Tarka Trail sign.

Cross the River Okement via a footbridge and go past some houses on your left to a road; turn right into Okehampton. After about 700 yards the road meets Fore Street at a T-junction; turn right to return to the White Hart.

🐾 THE TARKA TRAIL FROM OKEHAMPTON TO BELSTONE (2¹/₂ MILES)

To continue along the Trail, carry on past the White Hart and immediately beyond it turn left into a cobbled yard. Go past the Tourist Information Centre and the Museum of Dartmoor Life into a car park and turn left into Jacob's Pool. At the T-junction, turn right and follow Mill Road round to the left to the Town Mills. Go up the steps alongside the mill and turn sharp right into Courtenay Road.

At the end of the road go through a gate and across some fields to a wooded area. When the path emerges onto a track, turn left and at the junction right to follow a lane under the railway and the A30. About 300 yards beyond the road take a footpath on the right. When you reach the road at the end, turn right and follow it to Belstone.

At Belstone, take the lane south past the Tors pub and bear left across the grass at the end of the village to meet a track and follow it down into the valley. Go left at the bottom, cross a footbridge and go left again to join the next walk.

SOUTH ZEAL
The Oxenham Arms

ಆಜ್ಞಾ

This is a delightfully varied walk; it takes you through three picturesque villages, gives you a taste of the wide open expanses of Dartmoor and incorporates a particularly beautiful stretch of the Trail alongside the infant Taw, where Tarka fought over a rabbit with a band of stoats. You also have the chance to visit a fascinating 19th century water-powered forge. There is quite a long, steady climb up to the moor at the start, and parts of the route can become rather muddy after rain, so appropriate footwear is needed.

You are spoilt for choice on this walk. There are no fewer than five pubs along the route – two in South Zeal, one in Belstone, two in Sticklepath and one in South Tawton – all delightful places to stop. The Oxenham Arms, however, takes a lot of beating; for my money, it is the most charming old inn for many a mile, full of character and atmosphere.

Built in the late 12th century by lay monks, it is a solid granite building with the old beams and leaded windows one would expect in an edifice of that era. It has had a somewhat chequered history, having passed from the monks to the Burgoyne family, who used it as a dower house, and then to the Oxenhams from whom it takes its name, before being licensed – as long ago as 1477.

The main accommodation comprises a cosy bar with a magnificent granite fireplace, and a small family lounge with a 5,000-year-old monolith built into one of the walls. There is also a large garden and a delightful dining room, and overnight accommodation is available for those who want to linger.

Opening hours are 11 am to 2.30 pm and 6 pm to 11 pm on weekdays, 12 noon to 2.30 pm and 7 pm to 10.30 pm on Sundays; children are welcome in the garden and family room, and dogs are allowed. The food ranges from soup, paté, curry and salads to the pub's renowned steak, kidney, Guinness and mushroom pie. The resident ale is Dartmoor IPA (plus a guest ale which changes from time to time), and you will also find Tetley bitter, Carlsberg and Kronenbourg lager, Inch's Stonehouse cider, Murphy's stout and Guinness on draught. Telephone: 01837 840244.

- **GETTING THERE:** South Zeal is just south of the A30 between Okehampton and Exeter and is signposted from both directions.
- **PARKING:** There is a public car park at the eastern end of the village, and parking along the main street. There is a small forecourt in front of the pub, but it soon fills up and walkers are requested not to leave their cars there while walking.
- **LENGTH OF THE WALK:** $5^{1}/_{4}$ miles. Maps: OS Landranger 191 Okehampton and North Dartmoor; OS Outdoor Leisure 28 Dartmoor; OS Explorer 113 Okehampton (GR 651935).

THE WALK

1. Turn right and follow the main street of this lovely village for a few yards until you see a house called Mill Cottage on your right. Turn right just beyond it up a private drive and follow it to the right and to the left to reach a gate. Go through and keep to the left of the field beyond to another gate, which leads onto a lane. Turn right and follow the lane up to the main road.

Cross the road to another lane (signposted 'Bridlepath to the moor'). It climbs steeply, so take it gently and pause from time to time to

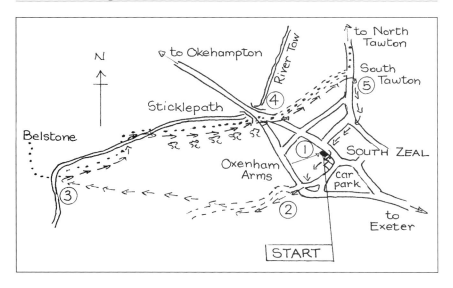

admire the wild flowers which abound in the hedgerows on either side in season. The lane deteriorates into a track and curves to the right. As it does so, you will see a path leading off straight ahead; follow that. It rejoins the track higher up; bear left, continuing to climb, and at the junction follow the main track round to the right. At the next two junctions, go left, following the signs to the moor. Go through a gate and continue climbing until you emerge onto the open moor. Look to the right as you do so and you will be rewarded for all your effort: the view over the lush mid-Devon countryside will take your breath away.

2. Follow the track across the moorland, and where it goes to the left go straight on through the gorse. You will soon meet up with another, less well-defined track; when this also goes to the left, continue straight on again. Although there is no path the going is relatively easy, and it does not matter if you deviate from your line slightly; you can always correct for it later.

It is beautifully peaceful up here, with the silence broken only by birdsong and the bleating of the sheep. As you come over the brow of the hill you will see the village of Belstone ahead of you. Make for that, aiming in the general direction of the church tower you can see towards the left of the village. As you go, you will see a large stone on your right, with 'DC1' inscribed on one side and 'SZ1' on the other. This is an ancient boundary stone marking the boundary between the warren lands of the Duke of Cornwall and those of the parish of South Zeal.

You will soon come to a rough path going in the same general direction in which you are heading. Follow it down the hill and then round a field to the right. Just beyond the field you come to a T-junction.

🐾 3. At this point there is a difference of opinion as to where the Tarka Trail goes. The Ordnance Survey map shows it running along the top of the valley on the other side of the River Taw, which would require you to cross the river and make your way up the hill. The official route, however, is alongside the river on the near bank, and this is by far the more attractive path anyway.

Turn right at the T-junction, therefore, and at the fork take the lower, left-hand path which goes down towards a fence on your left. You can hear the river below you, but the trees obscure it from view at this point. The path winds between the bracken and gorse and then goes into a wooded area and you can see the river at the bottom of a steep bank on your left. After ¼ mile you come to another fork; take the clearer path down towards the river and along the bank. This is a delightful spot, in amongst the trees, with the river bubbling along beside you.

Almost ½ mile after joining the Tarka Trail, you will find Ivy Tor towering above you on the right, and a little further on you will see a footbridge on your left. Cross it (signposted to Skaigh) and turn right to continue along the opposite bank. After 300 yards you will come to a junction; turn right (signposted to Sticklepath) and cross a footbridge to enter Skaigh Wood.

Go through a gate and follow the river through this lovely wood, with a mass of rhododendrons on your right and the lively river on your left. After about 600 yards you cross a stile, and after a little over ¼ mile more you will come to a track; turn left (signposted to Sticklepath and the A30). Go through a gate and after about 300 yards you will come to a road on the edge of Sticklepath – another very attractive village of stone and cob cottages. Turn left if you want to go into the village and visit Finch Foundry, a 19th-century water-powered forge which is now owned by the National Trust and is open to the public in summer, with fascinating demonstrations of the machinery at work.

4. To continue along the Tarka Trail, cross the road to a lane, following the cycle sign. After about 50 yards turn left up a green lane, signposted 'Tarka Trail'. It climbs steeply initially, but soon levels out. As it does so, you get an excellent view across the hedge on your right to Dartmoor. The hedgerows on either side are full of interest, with seasonal wild flowers and birds in abundance. The lane emerges at a road alongside the church and opposite the pub in South Tawton, yet another picture-postcard village.

5. This is where you leave the Trail; it goes left along the road, while your route takes you right. Follow the road out of the village, and at the first junction you come to, after about 300 yards, turn left (signposted to Dishcombe). After another 150 yards, turn right (signposted to South Zeal). This lane will bring you out almost opposite the Oxenham Arms.

THE TARKA TRAIL FROM SOUTH TAWTON TO NEWLAND CROSS (5¹/₄ MILES)

The Trail follows the road north out of South Tawton and across the A30 to Taw Green. At the junction here, follow the signs for North Tawton and North Wyke. At the T-junction go left and at the next, where the lane meets the B3215, turn right. After about 700 yards you will come to Newland Cross; the Trail follows a path to the left just beyond the junction – the route of the next walk.

NORTH TAWTON
The Fountain Inn

❧

Farm tracks, riverside paths, pretty woodland and hedgerows, beautiful views – this delightful walk has them all. This stretch of the Tarka Trail is never far from the gently flowing River Taw, now 'a proper river with bridges, brooks, islands and mills' as Williamson described it, and the route back to North Tawton shows off the countryside which inspired some of the late Poet Laureate Ted Hughes's work. (Hughes lived at North Tawton.) There is some steady climbing along the way, but none of it is too steep.

North Tawton was once a major centre of the wool trade, and although its influence has declined, it is still very proud of its status as a town rather than a village. The Fountain is an attractive 16th century coaching inn, which has just been refurbished. It is approached through the usual coaching inn archway, although the courtyard behind it has long since been blocked off. Instead, a pretty fountain faces you as you go in, with the bar on the right and a restaurant on the left, both attractively furnished and full of atmosphere. Children are welcome, but dogs are not allowed when food is being served.

There is an interesting array of beers and other drinks available; the draught offerings are Yeoman Bitter, Hicks Special, Daylight Robbery, Spitfire and Worthington Creamflow, plus Carlsberg, Stella Artois and Carling lager, Cheddar Valley cider and Guinness. The bar menu ranges from sandwiches and jacket potatoes to lasagne and scampi, and there is a separate restaurant menu. Opening hours are 11.30 am to 2.30 pm and 5.30 pm to 11 pm on Mondays to Fridays, 11.30 am to 4 pm and 6 pm to 11 pm on Saturdays and 12 noon to 4 pm and 7 pm to 10.30 pm on Sundays. Telephone: 01837 82551.

- **GETTING THERE:** The A3072 between Okehampton and Crediton runs just south of the town, which is clearly signposted from it. The Fountain Inn is in Exeter Street, which runs east from The Square in the town centre.
- **PARKING:** There is no pub car park, but you can usually find parking in the streets and roads nearby.
- **LENGTH OF THE WALK:** $6^1/_4$ miles. Maps: OS Landranger 191 Okehampton and North Dartmoor; OS Explorer 113 Okehampton (GR 664017).

THE WALK

1. Follow Exeter Street west to The Square and turn left into High Street. After 50 yards, turn right into Barton Street. Where this street turns to the right and becomes Barton Hill, go straight on along a path, following the public footpath sign. Cross a stile into a field and keep to the left, alongside a bank.

After a while the path bears right, diagonally across the field. Go through the gate at the end and bear right to cross the next field. You come out by a warehouse; follow the broad track which runs to the left of it and you will come out onto a road. Turn right, passing the lovely old 16th century manor house of The Barton and crossing two bridges.

2. Immediately beyond the second bridge, turn right to join the Tarka Trail. Go through a gate and follow the path to the right alongside the River Taw, which here flows gently and sedately between tree-fringed banks. At the end of the field, follow the path round to the left. The water is almost motionless along here, and the reason soon becomes clear as you pass a weir. After that it flows much more rapidly as it tumbles over the rocks below.

After a while you cross a wooden bridge and go through a rather

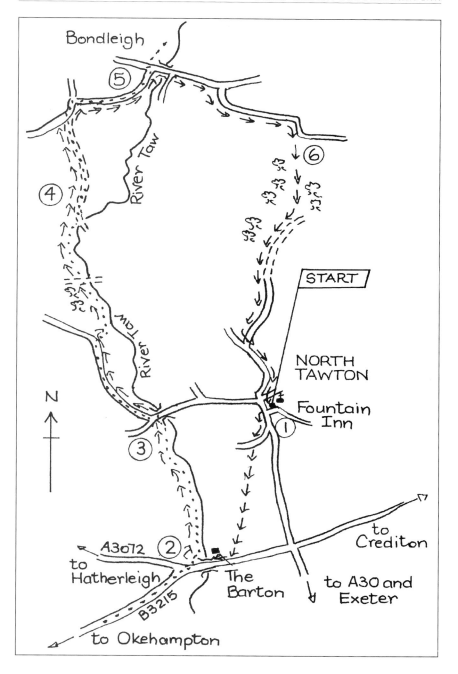

Bondleigh

⑤

River Taw

④

River Taw

N
↑

③

START

NORTH
TAWTON

Fountain
Inn
①

⑥

to
Crediton

A3072

②

to
Hatherleigh

B3215

The
Barton

to A30 and
Exeter

to Okehampton

dilapidated gate. Cross the field on the other side, keeping to the riverbank, and when it curves to the left, follow it round. When it bends to the right again, however, you should cut across the field to the road bridge you can see ahead of you.

3. Go through a turnstile and turn left along the road beyond, then immediately right into a quiet lane enclosed by hedges (signposted to Winkleigh). Follow this for a little over ¹/₂ mile, and when it bends sharply to the left, go right, following the Tarka Trail footpath sign. Cross the stile on your left, following the Tarka Trail waymark, rather than turning right to follow the other path.

You cross a stile after a while into a delightful wood, carpeted with flowers for much of the year, with the river flowing placidly beside you on the right. After about 300 yards you emerge via another stile onto a track. Cross it into a field and continue to follow the river. Where the river takes a sharp turn to the right, you will see a gate on your right; go through it and continue to follow the river to another gate. There is a footbridge on your right; ignore it and go down a short path to a green lane.

4. Turn left (signposted to Bondleigh) and follow the track as it climbs steadily between high hedges. This is a very peaceful stretch as you leave the river, the silence broken only by the susurration of the breeze through the trees and crops and the occasional distant bleating of a sheep.

After about 700 yards you join a metalled track. Go straight on, and as you do so you will get a very good view, particularly to your right. You pass a farm and then join a lane. Go straight on, and after a few yards follow the main lane round to the right (signposted to Bondleigh). The view across the valley as you go is typical of this part of Devon: small fields separated by hedges and interspersed with woods, with attractive old farmhouses dotted about. The lane curves to the left to run alongside the river, which along here is fringed by a mass of Himalayan balsam.

5. At the T-junction, turn right to cross Bondleigh Bridge (signposted to North Tawton); this is where you leave the Tarka Trail. At the junction immediately across the river, go straight on and follow the lane as it climbs steadily out of the valley. At the top you will come to a junction; turn right (signposted to Hill). You get another pretty view ahead and to your right. The lane descends to cross a small stream and then climbs again. At the top of the hill, you get a grand view to the right, all the way across to Dartmoor. You pass a farm and the lane bends sharp right.

6. After another 100 yards or so it bends to the left again; as it does so, go right through a gate into a field, following the public footpath sign. Go half right across the field to a stile leading into a wood (a rather superfluous stile as it happens, as there is no fence on either side). Follow the path through the wood on the other side, and at the other end cross a small rivulet and go up some steps to another stile.

The official route of the path on the other side is straight across, but the field can become rather neglected and overgrown, so you may prefer to swing right and keep to the wooded area, making your way round in a semicircle to the next stream. When you reach it, bear left to reach a footbridge across it and keep to the fence on the other side. At the end of the wood, cross a stile into a field and keep to the left. At the top, you get another good view, and then you begin to descend towards another wood. Towards the end of the field, you will find a gate on the left leading onto a track.

After a few yards, you join another track; turn right and climb gently through the wood. Go through a gate and the track continues to climb between high hedges. After 600 yards it joins a metalled lane; go straight on. After almost $1/2$ mile more it meets another lane at a T-junction on the outskirts of North Tawton; turn left to return to the town centre, and left again at the end of The Square for the Fountain Inn.

🐾 THE TARKA TRAIL FROM BONDLEIGH BRIDGE TO WESTACOTT WOOD (3 MILES)

The Trail goes left at the Bondleigh Bridge T-junction, and then right through a gate. It follows the river for a while and then goes left to a footbridge and on to a lane. It follows the lane to the right to a T-junction and then goes right again to join the B3220, where it turns right yet again. Immediately across the river it goes left onto a footpath.

After crossing several fields, it reaches a hedge and follows it round to the left to a green lane. It turns right here and eventually emerges into a field. There it goes left along a track to the river, which it follows to Westacott Wood. It skirts the wood to a road and turns left to cross the river again and join the route of the next walk.

WEMBWORTHY
The Lymington Arms

This is the final leg of the southern loop of the Tarka Trail, and a delightful stretch it is. Much of it is through a variety of different woodland, from deciduous to coniferous, from dense, closely packed undergrowth to light, airy rides. There are also a few farm paths and tracks to enjoy. To join the Trail, you follow a quiet, hedge-fringed lane, and the route back to the pub takes you along more of the same. There is some steady climbing in places, but you are rewarded for your efforts with superb views.

This is a pleasant inn, well known locally for its food and drink and for its friendly atmosphere. Built in 1820, it is nicely furnished and decorated, with its thick stone walls exposed in places, and an intriguing collection of jugs hanging from the beams in the lounge area. The accommodation comprises an open-plan bar and lounge area in the front, with a pool table in a side room, a large restaurant at the back and tables out on the grass beside the car park. Bed and breakfast accommodation is available, and both children and dogs are welcomed.

There are always three real ales on offer: Flowers Original, Brakspear Bitter and a guest beer which changes regularly. In addition, you will find Whitbread Trophy bitter, Heineken and Stella Artois lager, Stowford Press and Winkleigh cider, Farmers' Tipple scrumpy and Guinness on draught. The food is wide-ranging, from filled baguettes, ploughman's lunches and other bar snacks to a full restaurant menu and a three-course Sunday roast dinner. The chef is particularly noted for his authentic Indian curries. The pub is open from 12 noon to 2.30 pm or 3 pm (depending on demand) and 5.30 pm to 11 pm on Mondays to Saturdays and from 12 noon to 4 pm and 7 pm to 10.30 pm on Sundays. Telephone: 01837 83572.

- **GETTING THERE:** Turn south-west off the A377 Crediton to Barnstaple road at Eggesford and follow the signs to Wembworthy and Winkleigh. The pub is not in the village itself, but at a crossroads on the main road which bypasses it, so when the road forks, follow the sign for Winkleigh, not Wembworthy.
- **PARKING:** There is a large pub car park, and the licensee has no objection to customers leaving their cars there while they walk, as long as they ask first.
- **LENGTH OF THE WALK:** 7³/₄ miles. Maps: OS Landranger 191 Okehampton and North Dartmoor; OS Explorer 113 Okehampton (start and finish), 127 South Molton and Chulmleigh (middle section) (GR 663092).

THE WALK

1. Turn left outside the pub and left again (signposted to Brushford and Coldridge). You pass some cottages and go downhill to cross a small stream. There are a few more cottages on the other side and the lane begins to climb gently between high hedges. After just over ¹/₂ mile you will come to a crossroads. Go straight across (signposted to Coldridge) and you will soon get a very good view over the undulating farmland across the hedges ahead of you, and all the way to Dartmoor on your right. The lane then begins to descend into the valley of the River Taw.

2. About a mile after the crossroads, you will see a Tarka Trail signpost pointing left across a stile. Leave the lane to join the Trail and cross a field to a footbridge and then another stile. Bear left on the other side to a gate in the far corner of the field, and bear left across the next field to skirt some ruined farm buildings and follow the hedge at the top of the field to a wood.

There is a clear track between a conifer plantation on the left and a deciduous wood on the right, stretching down to the River Taw. When

57

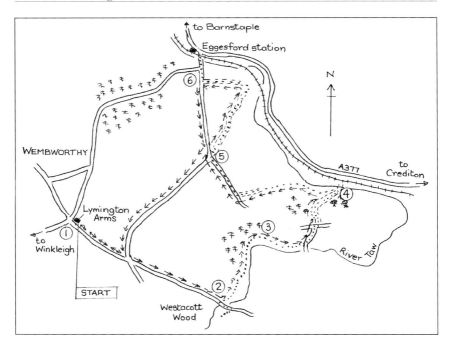

the main track bends to the right towards the river, go straight on through a gate, following the public footpath sign. This leads to a grassy track between the conifer plantation and a meadow beside the river. After a while the track goes to the left; go right, following the Tarka Trail sign, and then immediately left again to join a path alongside a bank on the edge of the wood. You can hear the river down on the right, but it is hidden by trees at this point.

You cross a stream and the path bends to the right and becomes a little less marked than it was as the bracken closes in from the left.

3. At the end of the wood you go through a gate into a meadow. Cross it to a stile and keep to the left of the next field. After a few yards you come to a gate; go through it into another field, and follow the right-hand hedge to another gate into a lane. Bear left.

The lane climbs steadily and at the top of the rise it bends sharply to the left to a T-junction. Turn right and then almost immediately left into a farmyard, following the Tarka Trail sign. Go down the surfaced track through the farm, and at the bottom turn left through a gate onto another track. This leads into a lovely deciduous wood, which slopes steeply into the valley on the left. It then swings to the right along the edge of a conifer plantation before taking a turn to the left again into the wood, descending fairly steeply. At the fork, take the left-hand route, following the main track downhill towards the river.

4. Just before you come to a bridge, turn left through a gate into a field, following the Tarka Trail sign, and go right to follow the field round, alongside the river. It is a long field, and at the end you go through a dilapidated gate. The river bends to the right here, but you go straight across the field to cross a small stream and bear left round a stand of trees to reach a gate leading onto a track.

Follow the track uphill between the trees on the left and a hedge on the right. Go through a gate at the top and between the farm buildings to a lane. Turn right and follow the lane.

5. After 600 yards or so you will come to a T-junction; turn right (signposted to Eggesford Station) and then immediately right again through a gate, following the Tarka Trail sign. Follow the track on the other side and you get another good view half left. Go through a gateway and follow the track along the edge of the next field; at the fork near the end, go left, away from the fence. You meet a hedge on the right; keep following it round to the right and then to the left. Cross a stile and go to the right to skirt the next field to a track; follow it to the left, past a church to a gate into a lane. At the junction go straight on.

6. About 150 yards further on, you will come to a T-junction. To complete the Tarka Trail, turn right and after 300 yards you will come to the railway section of the Trail, the Tarka Line, at Eggesford Station. To continue the walk back to the Lymington Arms, turn left and follow the lane as it climbs steadily to the Eggesford Fourways junction. Go straight on (signposted to Brushford and Winkleigh). After about $1^{1}/_{4}$ miles you will come to a crossroads; turn right (signposted to Wembworthy) to rejoin the lane you came out on. Follow it for a little over $^{1}/_{2}$ mile and you will find the pub on your right.

🐾 THE TARKA TRAIL FROM EGGESFORD STATION TO BARNSTAPLE (20 MILES)

From Eggesford Station the official Trail continues by train to Barnstaple.

BISHOP'S TAWTON
The Chichester Arms
❦

The views along this route are superb – at times it seems as though the whole of North Devon is laid out before you. Unfortunately, such pleasures have to be earned, and there are one or two stiff climbs to negotiate. The Tarka Trail follows the course of the Landkey Brook, a tributary of the River Taw, up which Tarka travelled after being separated from his mate. It makes its way to the nearby village of Landkey through a mixture of woodland and farm fields, and the route back to Bishop's Tawton is along pretty, peaceful lanes.

This is a delightful old inn beside the village green, with an attractive collection of period cottages and houses clustered around it. Built in the 15th century, it has the thick stone walls of the period, mostly plastered but with the stone exposed at one end of the long bar. In addition to this room, with its dark beams and large fireplace, there is an eating area and a family room, both very pleasantly furnished, a small courtyard at the back and a few tables at the front, where you can sit and watch the village going about its business. The inn is said to be haunted by a ghost, known as the lavender lady because of the distinctive scent that precedes her appearances.

The Chichester Arms is open all day, seven days a week, from 11.30 am on weekdays and from 12 noon on Sundays, and children are welcome everywhere except in the bar. Dogs, however, are not allowed. There are two regular ales – Dartmoor and Burton – and a wide variety of other drinks on tap: Tetley and Ansells bitters, Calder's Premium Cream Beer, Blackthorn cider, Carlsberg, Carlsberg Export and Castlemaine lager and Guinness. The food is equally varied, ranging from sandwiches and jacket potatoes to specials such as curry, fresh trout and spaghetti Bolognese. Telephone: 01271 343945.

- **GETTING THERE:** Bishop's Tawton straddles the A377 Barnstaple to Crediton road. The pub is in The Square; to reach it, turn east off the main road along Village Street.
- **PARKING:** There is a pub car park on the opposite side of the road. There is no objection to customers leaving their cars there while they walk, but do please ask first.
- **LENGTH OF THE WALK:** 4^1/$_2$ miles. Maps: OS Landranger 180 Barnstaple and Ilfracombe; OS Explorer 139 Bideford, Ilfracombe and Barnstaple (GR 567300).

THE TARKA TRAIL FROM BARNSTAPLE TO BISHOP'S TAWTON (2^1/$_2$ MILES)

Go right out of Barnstaple Station, and then left at the roundabout. At the next roundabout go right to cross the river. Turn sharp right on the other side to join a footpath alongside the river. Where the road bears left, bear right to keep to the riverbank. Pass under the A39 and at the fork in the path go left. When the Trail joins the A377, turn right and follow the road into Bishop's Tawton. Turn left up School Lane and follow a footpath to Easter Street; turn right to meet Walk 13 at Sentry Lane.

THE WALK

1. Sentry Lane runs west from The Square, along the side of the pub. Follow it up a hill and out of the village. At the top you get a very good view both ahead and behind you, and also to your left. As the lane bends to the right, go straight on across a stile, following the

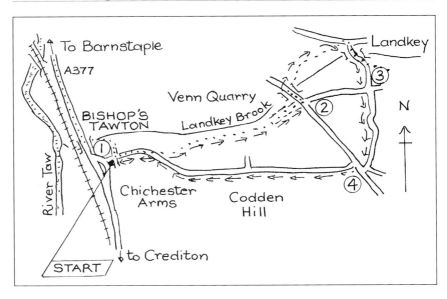

Tarka Trail sign. Bear left on the other side to a gap in the hedge ahead, and bear left again across the next field to a stile. As you go, you will see the spoil tips of the enormous Venn Quarry across the valley on your left.

Go to the left to skirt the next field, alongside the Landkey Brook, which here is audible but hidden from view by a fringe of trees. You will come to a path leading into the trees; take that and you will shortly come to a stile. Cross a rather muddy stretch beyond to another stile and a junction; go straight on, following the Tarka Trail sign. This stretch is usually a mass of wild flowers, depending on the season; the rosebay willowherb makes a particularly splendid display in late summer. The path winds in and out of the trees, and although it is still not visible, the chattering of the brook accompanies you as you follow it.

At the path junction go straight on, following the permissive path sign, rather than left via the quarry. After a few yards turn right across a stile and then a few yards beyond that left onto a track. Soon a lovely vista opens up ahead of you, across Landkey to rolling hills and a patchwork of fields and woods.

2. The track ends at a gate with a stile alongside; cross it to a lane and turn left (signposted to Venn and Barnstaple). Cross the brook and immediately on the other side turn right across a stile into a very pretty wood opposite it. Soon the path veers left away from the brook and you cross a stile to leave the wood. The path now runs between a fence on the right and a mass of brambles and bracken on the left, and you can see Landkey church ahead of you. Cross another stile and continue along the path, this time with a field on your left. You emerge onto a road; turn right into Landkey. After about 100 yards or so turn right again into Bableigh Road to leave the village.

3. You cross the brook and the lane swings left. When it swings right again, the Tarka Trail goes straight on into a field; you, however, should follow the lane round. It climbs quite steeply to a crossroads; go straight on (signposted to Bableigh), and continue the long, steady climb.

The banks alongside the lane are high and topped with hedges, blocking out the view for much of the time, but they provide a haven for wildlife and flowers. And when you get to the top of the hill, where the lane bends to the right and then the left, you are rewarded with the most superb views through the gateways: to the west over the valley to the quarry, to the south to the long mass of Codden Hill, to the north across Landkey to the open country beyond and to the east across the rich, undulating farmland. The lane then descends gently, past a farm, to a T-junction.

4. Turn sharp right (signposted to Venn and Bishop's Tawton), and 50 yards further on branch off to the left (signposted to Codden and Bishop's Tawton). This new lane goes downhill for a while and then levels off to skirt the bottom of Codden Hill. As you follow it along this straight stretch, you get a better view of the great gash of the quarry scarring the hillside opposite. The banks on either side of the lane, however, are full of wild flowers, and after a while you get a grand view across the valley of the River Taw ahead of you.

After $3/4$ mile you will come to a junction. Go straight on (signposted to Bishop's Tawton and Barnstaple), and after another 600 yards of almost dead-straight walking, the lane swings to the right, to the left and to the right again in quick succession. It then goes left again, passing the path you took on the way out, and descends into Bishop's Tawton.

LANDKEY
The Ring o' Bells

As an introduction to the lush, rolling farmland of North Devon, this section of the Tarka Trail takes a lot of beating. It follows field paths, farm tracks and quiet lanes up an attractive little valley, and our route then returns to Landkey via more pretty lanes. There is one quite long climb up the valley, but it is generally fairly gentle and the views, especially on the return journey, are wonderful.

The Ring o' Bells is an excellent pub: warm, friendly, full of character and with the kind of good-value traditional food local people travel some way to enjoy. The menu ranges from regulars like sandwiches, salads and sausages to daily specials like pork chops and roasts. It is a tribute to the quality of the cooking that the pub is full most lunchtimes.

The building dates back to the 15th century, and like many village inns was originally built to accommodate the workers who were building the church next door. It comprises a large panelled and beamed bar with bench seats round the walls and a games room (pool and skittles) off it, and a plush, snug little lounge with a large stone fireplace. Children are allowed in the games room, and dogs are welcome.

Marston's Pedigree, Welsh Bitter and Boddingtons are on tap, as well as two Whitbread offerings – Best and Trophy – Stella Artois and Heineken lagers, Murphy's stout and Merrydown cider. The inn is open from 11.30 am to 2.30 pm and 6.30 pm to 11 pm from Monday to Saturday, and at the usual more restricted Sunday hours. Telephone: 01271 830364.

- **GETTING THERE:** The village is just south of the A361 between Barnstaple and South Molton, and is clearly signposted from that road. Shortly before you reach the village centre you will pass the Methodist church on your left and see a war memorial cross on a corner on your right; turn sharp right here into Manor Road and follow it almost to the end of the village. The pub is just next to the church on the right.
- **PARKING:** There is no pub car park, but you should have no difficulty finding parking in the road outside.
- **LENGTH OF THE WALK:** 6½ miles. Maps: OS Landranger 180 Barnstaple and Ilfracombe; OS Outdoor Leisure 9 Exmoor (GR 591311).

THE WALK

1. Follow Manor Road past the church and take the first lane on the left to join the Tarka Trail (signposted to Bableigh). Cross the Landkey Brook and follow the lane round to the left. When it bends to the right, go straight on across a stile, following the Tarka Trail sign. Bear right slightly on the other side to reach a gate and keep to the hedge on your left beyond it to a stile. Go straight across the next field to a gate leading onto a lane.

Go left and follow the lane round to the right. At the T-junction, turn left and at the crossroads about 50 yards further on go straight across into Tanner's Lane. You pass some new houses and cross a stream.

2. Immediately on the other side, turn left through a kissing gate, following the Tarka Trail sign. Skirt round to the left of a football field, following a stream. After about 100 yards or so, you will find a stile on your left with a footbridge on the other side. Cross both and bear right along the other bank.

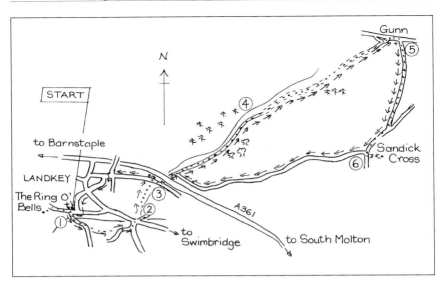

You will find another stile on your left; cross it and bear right across the field beyond to yet another stile in the hedge ahead. Cross the next field to another stile leading onto a lane. As you do so, you get a lovely view over the gentle hills and rich farmland.

3. Turn right at the lane, and after about 70 yards left (signposted to Hurscott, Birch and Gunn). Pass under the busy A361 road and at the junction on the other side go straight on (signposted to Birch). This is a typical Devon lane of high banks and flower-filled hedges in season, and because it is a dead end it is delightfully peaceful, with virtually no traffic.

You climb gently but steadily up the valley, with the stream invisible beyond the trees on your left. After 700 yards or so you enter a pretty wood, and from time to time you can just see the stream meandering quietly along through the trees.

4. About a mile after passing under the A361, the lane comes to an end and becomes a metalled track; carry straight on, past a pretty whitewashed cottage, climbing more steeply now. The track curves right, away from the stream, and then left again between some farm buildings. When it turns right again, go straight on through a gate into a field, following the bridleway sign. Keep to the top of the field and you get a pleasant view across the valley to a patchwork of fields and hedges. There is a gate at the end of the field; go across the top of the next field to another gate leading into a green lane.

Pass a small conifer plantation and cross a small stream into a field. Go through a gate on the other side into another green lane. This climbs to another gate leading into a field. Keep to the left alongside the hedge and you will join a track; bear right, still keeping to the left-hand side of the field. When the track swings left through a gate, follow it round, and when it joins another track, go straight on, You pass a number of cottages and come to a T-junction; turn right and at the next T-junction right again.

5. Turn right down a lane beyond the church (signposted to Swimbridge). Look out through the gateways on your right from time to time for another grand view of the green hills rolling away into the distance. This is another pretty, peaceful lane, with just the birdsong or the occasional sounds of farm life blown on the breeze to disturb the silence. The Trail follows it for $3/4$ mile to a T-junction; turn right (signposted to Yarnacott and Swimbridge). As you go, another excellent view opens up ahead.

6. After another 400 yards, you come to a junction. This is where you leave the Tarka Trail; it goes straight on for a few yards and then left, while you turn right, following the sign for Landkey. There are more delightful views to be enjoyed over the hedges on the right along this stretch. After a mile or so, the hedge gives way to a low bank for a while, and a magnificent panorama opens up to the right, and also, as the lane begins to descend, ahead of you over Landkey to the farms and woods beyond.

At the bottom of the hill, the lane runs parallel to the A361 for a short distance to a junction. This is where you meet your outbound route; follow the main lane round to the left and pass under the main road. At the T-junction turn right (signposted to Harford) and carry straight on past the point where you came across the fields on your outward journey. At the crossroads, go straight on (signposted to Barnstaple). About 100 yards further on, turn left down a narrow lane and follow it round to the right. At the next crossroads, go straight across into Vicarage Road, and at the T-junction at the bottom turn right into Manor Road to return to the pub.

THE TARKA TRAIL FROM SANDICK CROSS TO CHERITON (21 MILES)

There are virtually no services and very little human habitation along the Trail as it winds up to Exmoor and then crosses the moor towards the coast. From Sandick Cross it goes east along a track to a lane which leads into West Buckland; at the T-junction in the village the Trail goes left and then right along a footpath. It crosses farm fields to a lane, which it follows eastwards, across a crossroads to East Buckland and on to a T-junction, where it goes right to another T-junction at Blakewell.

Here it goes right again and then left onto a footpath which leads down into the valley of the River Bray. It follows the river through a wood and then climbs a hill to Grasspark. It goes through the farm to a lane and right to reach the A399. It crosses the road and then, when the lane bends sharply to the right, turns left along a track into a wood. It continues to follow forest tracks until it emerges onto a lane.

It goes left along the lane for a short distance, and then takes a path on the left up a hill and through a farm to another lane. It follows this lane right for a while, before branching off to the left again, along a track into a wood. It emerges from the wood to climb a steep hill to yet another lane; it follows this to the right, through a farm, and on the other side bears left onto a path which goes north-east to cross Whitefield Down.

On the other side of the Down, it joins a road and follows it to the left until the road takes a sharp turn to the left at the Sloley Stone. Here it goes off to the right, following a track and then a field boundary to the B3358. It crosses the road and continues to keep to the boundary for a mile to Woodbarrow Gate. Here it turns sharp right and follows a new path south-east to Exe Head.

There it goes left through a gate and follows the path along a bank for a while and then left into a valley. It crosses the stream at the bottom and follows it downstream, crossing it again at Hoar Oak Tree. After some distance it leaves the stream to follow a field boundary up the hill and round a corner to a track. This leads to Cheriton.

LYNMOUTH
The Rising Sun Hotel

❦

This is where the Tarka Trail leaves the wastes of Exmoor proper, and follows leaping rivers in which Tarka fought his deadly enemy, the hound Deadlock, to the coast. And a more magnificent route would be hard to find, combining as it does a densely wooded valley and a high ridge which offers the most superb views imaginable. The walk to the Trail is equally beautiful, following the lovely East Lyn River upstream through more lush woodland. There are a few climbs, some fairly steep, but the rewards are spectacular.

This beautiful, whitewashed 14th century building, set on a path a little above Riverside Road, was originally a row of fishermen's cottages and still retains something of their character. Long and narrow, it comprises two main rooms, a bar and a restaurant. The bar has mainly bare stone walls, while those of the restaurant are panelled. Both rooms have attractive leaded windows overlooking the bustle of Riverside Road.

Opening hours vary according to the season. During school summer holidays, the pub is open all day, from 11 am to 11 pm. For the rest of the summer it closes in the afternoon between 3 pm and 6.30 pm, and in winter between 2.30 pm and 6.30 pm. Sunday hours are 12 noon to 3 pm (12 noon to 2.30 pm in winter) and 7 pm to 10.30 pm. Children are allowed in the restaurant but not in the bar; dogs in the bar but not in the restaurant. However, if you have both, do not despair – there are a couple of tables where both are allowed together.

Bar snacks are available at midday, ranging from ploughman's lunches and soups to such fish delicacies as cod in a beer batter, moules marinières and crab. In the evenings a full restaurant menu is offered but no bar food. The regular real ales are Exmoor Gold and Bass (summer only), and Exmoor Fox and Exmoor Ale (all year), and Tetley Smooth bitter, Ind Coope Pale Ale, Carlsberg and Stella Artois lager, Dry Blackthorn and Scrumpy Jack cider and Guinness are also served. Accommodation is available for those who want to stay and explore this lovely part of Devon further. Telephone: 01598 753223.

- **GETTING THERE:** The village is on the A39 between Ilfracombe and Porlock. The Rising Sun is in Riverside Road, which runs down to the harbour from the main road.
- **PARKING:** There is no pub parking. The most convenient public car park is at the Esplanade, at the end of Riverside Road. You may find parking in the street if you are there between 31 October and Easter, but during the summer on-street parking is restricted to two hours at a time.
- **LENGTH OF THE WALK:** 7 miles. Maps: OS Landranger 180 Barnstaple and Ilfracombe; OS Outdoor Leisure 9 Exmoor (GR 722496).

THE WALK

1. Follow Riverside Road away from the harbour, with the River Lyn on your left, to the main road. Cross it and go down some steps to a path alongside a car park. The river beside you is now the East Lyn, having parted company with its western sister just before the road. When you see a white footbridge on your left, do not cross it but continue along the path by the riverside. After $1/4$ mile you will come to another bridge; cross this one (signposted to Watersmeet) and turn right to continue up the other bank.

At the fork in the path immediately on the other side take the right-hand path, which continues to follow the river. It is idyllic along here, with the river bubbling along beside you, the steep, densely wooded

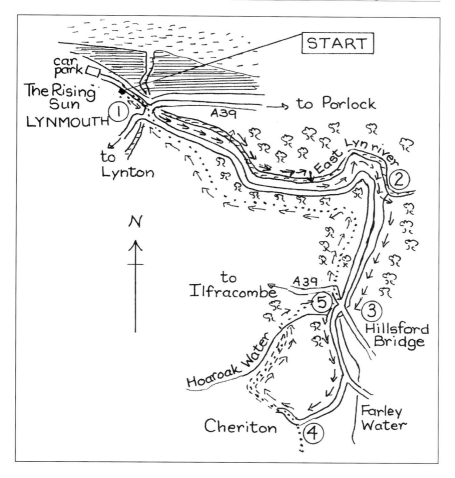

hillsides stretching up on either side, and an array of wild flowers lining the path in summer. When you come to another fork; go right alongside the river again, following the sign for Watersmeet.

The path climbs high above the river for a while and then you come to another bridge; cross again and continue upstream on the other side. At the next bridge, which is signposted to Countisbury, do not cross but carry straight on. The path eventually emerges onto a track; bear left and follow it round to the right. When it swings left to cross a bridge, go straight on. Soon you will see Watersmeet House, a pretty Victorian fishing lodge which is now a National Trust restaurant, across the river on your left.

2. The path climbs slightly and at the top, where it forks, go left to cross Hoaroak Water, a tributary of the East Lyn. Immediately on the other side go sharp right up some steps (signposted to Hillsford Bridge). If you want to avoid the steps, there is another path which goes round to the left; just make sure that you end up on the path to Hillsford Bridge, as there are several paths and signs in this fairly constricted area. The path climbs high above the water, with the dense wood on either side. It is a fairly stiff climb, but after a while it levels off somewhat.

3. You emerge from the wood through a gate onto a road at Hillsford Bridge; turn right to cross the river and then immediately left up a lane (signposted to Bridge Ball, Cheriton and Scoresdown). It takes you into a wood alongside Farley Water and then, after about 600 yards, curves right, away from the river, and climbs out of the wood.

At the junction, go straight on (signposted to Cheriton) and continue climbing. It is a steep climb, but you are rewarded at the top with a grand view over the wooded valley to the barren moorland beyond.

4. Follow the lane past some cottages and farm buildings, and where it bends to the right you join the Tarka Trail, which here follows the route of the Two Moors Way. Indeed, at the bend there is a sign indicating that this is the direction of the Two Moors Way. At the next bend, follow the lane round to the right again (signposted to Scoresdown and Lyn Down) and then to the left.

It peters out and becomes a rough track; continue along that as it swings to the right and begins to descend to the valley of Hoaroak Water. At the bottom go left past some cottages to cross the river, and turn immediately right through a gate into a wood on the other side. There is a sign just beyond the gate, indicating that this is the Two Moors Way and also pointing to Watersmeet, but it is not immediately obvious. At the fork follow the track on the right, beside the river (signposted simply 'bridleway').

After a short, pretty stretch through the wood along the riverbank the track becomes a path and goes to the left to avoid a hotel. You go through a gate and after a little while come to a junction; go straight on (signposted for the woodland walk to the National Trust car park). Go through another gate and turn right to cross the top of a field. At the end is yet another gate leading into a wood. You emerge from the wood onto a drive; turn left and follow it down to join the A39 back at Hillsford Bridge.

5. Turn left and follow the road for 100 yards; when it swings sharply left, go straight on up a track (signposted to East Lyn and Lynmouth). This takes you through a gate and into some trees, and climbs steadily up the hillside, with the wood falling steeply to the river far below you on the right. After a while you emerge from the trees and pass the Myrtleberry South Iron Age camp. You get a grand view ahead and to your right over the woods and moors.

At the path junction go straight on (signposted to Lynton and Lynmouth). You go through another stretch of woodland and when you emerge again, the view will take your breath away: on a clear day you can see across the farms and the sea to the Welsh coast and even the Brecon Beacons in the distance. At the next fork go straight on again (again signposted to Lynton and Lynmouth).

You go through two gates in quick succession and the path twists and turns as it descends to cross a small stream and then climbs up the other side, still twisting. As you reach the top, you get a good view up the East Lyn gorge to the moors as well as the panorama across the Bristol Channel to Wales, which is still with you. The path begins to descend again, and you may be relieved to know that this descent will not be followed by another climb. At the junction at Oxen Tor turn right (signposted to Lynmouth). You can now see the village tucked under the hill on your left, with Lynton above it. You come to a fork; go right, down the hill and into a wood. At the next junction, go straight on (signposted to Lynmouth). When you reach the village, you emerge onto a surfaced path between houses which leads to a road. Turn left and at the T-junction right, then left again along Riverside Road.

🐾 THE TARKA TRAIL FROM LYNMOUTH TO GIRT DOWN (9½ MILES)

The Trail now joins the South West Coast Path. It climbs some steps towards the end of the Esplanade, just before the cliff railway, and then winds up the hill behind Lynmouth. It follows a road and path along the coast to the Valley of the Rocks. Here it joins a road, which it follows for about 1½ miles before turning off right to take a track to a lane.

When the lane makes a hairpin bend, the Trail leaves it to follow a path along the coast. It turns inland at Heddon's Mouth to cross the river, then after some zigzagging heads back to the coast. It then follows a path parallel to the coast past Neck Wood and across Holdstone Down, turning inland to cross Sherrydown before heading coastwards again to reach Girt Down.

COMBE MARTIN
The Pack o' Cards

Magnificent panoramas are the main features of this walk: the undulating contours of the rich North Devon farmland rolling away to the south and the rugged coastline to east and west, with the empty expanse of open sea to the north. The Tarka Trail follows the South West Coast Path through the north-western corner of Exmoor, and the route to it consists mainly of pretty paths and green lanes, sometimes sunk below high banks, sometimes more open, but always full of interest. There is some stiff climbing to reach the Trail, but once there the going is relatively easy.

The Pack o' Cards has a strange name and a fascinating history. It was built in 1690 by one George Ley to celebrate his gambling successes, and was designed with a pack of playing cards in mind. So there are four floors to represent the four suits, 13 doors on each floor for the cards in each suit, 52 stairs (and originally 52 windows) for the total number of cards in the pack, etc.

It is a delightful pub with a warm, panelled bar, a more basic pool bar, an attractive restaurant, a light, airy conservatory and a large, pretty garden with a children's adventure playground. An interesting feature is the small museum which explains the background to the building and its design.

In summer the pub is open from 11 am to 11 pm (12 noon to 10.30 pm on Sundays), and in winter from 11.30 am to 2.30 pm and 6.30 pm to 11 pm (10.30 pm on Sundays). Children are welcome, and dogs are allowed in winter but not in summer, as they can become a bit of a nuisance when the pub is full. Accommodation is available for those wanting to stay a little longer.

The food is all home-made, from local produce, and ranges from soups, jacket potatoes, ploughman's lunches and sandwiches to chicken, steak and fish dishes, as well as a range of vegetarian offerings. The draught tipples are Bass, Directors, Worthington, Bass Special, Worthington Creamflow, Caffrey's, Guinness, Carling and Grolsch lagers and Strongbow cider. Delicious cream teas are also available. Telephone: 01271 882300.

- **GETTING THERE:** Combe Martin is on the A399 between Ilfracombe and Lynton. The pub is in High Street, the main street of the village (at 2 miles reputed to be the longest in England).
- **PARKING:** There is a large pub car park and there is no objection to customers leaving their cars there while they walk, provided they ask first.
- **LENGTH OF THE WALK:** 4 miles. Maps: OS Landranger 180 Barnstaple and Ilfracombe; OS Outdoor Leisure 9 Exmoor (GR 583467).

THE WALK

1. Turn right into High Street from the Pack o' Cards and then take the first turning left, just beyond the post office, into Chapel Lane. At the junction with Highfield Gardens, follow the main lane round to the right. Keep to the main lane again at the next junction (Holland Avenue), climbing up the valley side.

Where the lane ends turn left up a track between high banks, which soon narrows to a path, still climbing. The path crosses a track; go straight on, and straight on again where it crosses the track again. The climb here is rather steep, and it can be somewhat muddy at times, but when you reach the top you begin to enjoy the superb views which are such a feature of this walk.

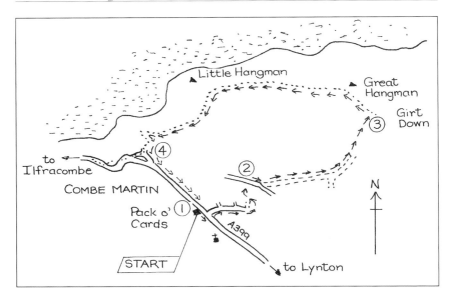

2. The path emerges onto a lane; turn right, following the footpath sign to Great Hangman via Knapdown Lane, and after 50 yards turn left up a green lane (again signposted to Great Hangman via Knapdown Lane). As the green lane climbs, the high banks and hedges cut out any views on either side, but it is worth stopping from time to time to enjoy the outlook to the sea behind you. And towards the top, as the hedge opens up, there is a lovely view of the gorse- and heather-covered moorland along the coast to the left.

At the top of the climb, the path levels off and curves to the right to join a track; turn left (signposted to Great Hangman). Where the main track turns to the left, go straight on past a house and through a gate. This new track passes some farm buildings and goes through a gateway before swinging left; follow it round and you now get a superb view: to the sea on the left, over the open moorland on the right and across farms and woods behind you. Go through another gate, then an empty gateway and another gate, all in quick succession, and bear right across the field beyond to yet another gate. Cross the stile alongside and follow the wall on the right. Where it bends to the right, cut straight along a grassy track to cut off the corner.

3. At the next corner turn left along a broad path, following the Coast Path sign. You are now on the Tarka Trail, which along here follows the same route as the South West Coast Path. This area is beautiful in late summer when the yellow of the gorse mingles with the purple of the heather. As you climb to Great Hangman, you get a magnificent view to the right of the coast with its sheer cliffs and the open moorland above, and behind you is an attractive patchwork of fields and hedges.

At the top a new panorama opens up, with the coast stretching into the distance ahead in a succession of coves and cliffs. Follow the path down the other side to a stile, keeping that magnificent view along the coast, with Little Hangman in the foreground. The path goes round the edge of a field and you go through a gate and along the top of a cliff.

You pass Little Hangman, keeping to the wall as indicated by the Coast Path sign. The path descends steeply and goes through a belt of trees. It passes an attractive cove and swings right around it to a stile. At the junction on the other side go straight on, following the Coast Path sign to Combe Martin. There is a short climb up a hill ahead and you begin your descent back to Combe Martin. You pass a shelter and enter some trees again. The path swings to the left and there is a long straight stretch before it swings right again down some steps to a track. The track goes to the right and joins a lane; turn left and follow the lane down to a car park.

4. This is where you leave the Tarka Trail, which bears right to join the main road out of Combe Martin. At the end of the car park you should turn left along Cross Street, passing the Motor Cycle Museum, an interesting collection of old machines, as you go. At the junction at the end, turn left and follow the main street (which changes name from time to time, although you are unlikely to notice) for about 750 yards back to the Pack o' Cards.

THE TARKA TRAIL FROM COMBE MARTIN TO SANDY COVE (1/2 MILE)

The Trail climbs out of Combe Martin along the A399 before turning right along a lane. It rejoins the A399 higher up and follows it, turning right to Sandy Cove at the Berrynarbor turning.

BERRYNARBOR
Ye Olde Globe

Stunning views, quiet woods, secluded coves, chiselled cliffs – this part of the Trail, which follows the route of the South West Coast Path, has them all and more. And the route back to Berrynarbor from the Trail is a delightful ramble along pretty lanes, with more superb views along the way. There are some stiff climbs, especially along the coast, but the views more than justify the effort.

This lovely, characterful pub is said to date back to the 13th century and, like so many village pubs, originated as a row of cottages to house men working on the nearby church. It still has the blackened beams and low ceilings of the period, and the lime ash floor dates back 400 years.

The main bar is decorated with old farm implements and has a couple of snug little alcoves, under one of which is the old village well. There is also an attractive lounge with a large stone fireplace and antique weapons on the walls, a very pleasant dining room, also with a large stone fireplace, and a pretty garden. The family room is a delight for children, with a skittle alley and an exciting play area attached.

Both children and dogs are welcomed, and the pub is open every day from 11.30 am to 2.30 pm and 6 pm to 11 pm (7 pm to 11 pm in winter). The award-winning food ranges from ploughman's lunches to steak, pasta, chilli and vegetarian main courses. Being an Ushers house, it has Ushers Best and Directors on tap, as well as John Smith's, Courage mild, Carlsberg, Stella Artois and Heineken lagers, Scrumpy Jack and Blackthorn ciders and Guinness. Telephone: 01271 882465.

- **GETTING THERE:** Turn south off the A399 between Combe Martin and Ilfracombe, following the signs to Berrynarbor.
- **PARKING:** The forecourt in front of the pub is very small, so cars should not be left there while you are walking. You are requested to use the free public car park, which is clearly signposted at the eastern end of the village.
- **LENGTH OF THE WALK:** 6 miles. Maps: OS Landranger 180 Barnstaple and Ilfracombe; OS Explorer 139 Bideford, Ilfracombe and Barnstaple; OS Outdoor Leisure 9 Exmoor (GR 560467).

THE WALK

1. Take the road out of Berrynarbor towards Combe Martin. If you are starting from the Olde Globe, turn left and at the junction follow the main lane round to the left; from the car park return to the main lane through the village and turn right. The lane climbs through the straggling outskirts of the village, and as you go, you can look back for a good view up Sterridge Valley.

2. The lane emerges at the main A399 and you get your first view of the coast beyond Combe Martin. This is where you join the Tarka Trail, which follows the same route as the South West Coast Path along this stretch. Cross the road and go through a gap in a fence, following the direction of the Coast Path sign. Take a shady lane to the Sandy Cove Hotel. At the junction, cross the road and follow the lane that goes half left, above the hotel, following the Coast Path sign and the Tarka Trail waymark.

The lane passes the hotel and some houses and then becomes a track as it enters a pretty wood, with the sea down on the right. When the trees thin out, you can see across Combe Martin Bay to the steep slopes of Little Hangman. You pass a campsite on your left and towards the

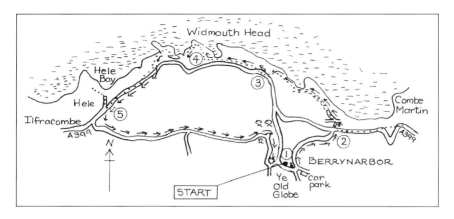

end you will see a Coast Path sign pointing right. Leave the track here and go through the gate and down some steps into another campsite. Follow the right-hand boundary as requested by the sign near the gate, down the field and round to the left. Cross a stile and keep to the right-hand edge of the next field to another stile followed by a footbridge.

3. This brings you out on the A399; turn right. Cross the entrance to Watermouth Cove caravan park and follow the footpath on the other side, which runs alongside the road with a fence on either side. After 200 yards or so, the path emerges onto the road itself at Watermouth Castle, a popular theme park. Turn right.

A few yards further on, just opposite the entrance to the castle, you have a choice, depending on the tide. At low tide, you can turn right, off the road and go down to the water, climbing up after a short distance into a small wood. At high tide, that option is not open to you – you need to follow the road for about 150 yards until you find a stile on your right, and cross that, bearing left along the path through the wood.

4. You eventually leave the wood, and the path turns right alongside a field. Cross a stile at the end and go down some steps. Bear right, as indicated by the Coast Path sign; as you go, you get a good view across the bay to the slopes of Exmoor above Combe Martin. The path goes round to the left and you get another pretty view back up Water Mouth. There is a steep climb up some steps to Widmouth Head, but when you get to the top the views are quite stunning, both ahead and behind you.

Samson's Bay

You go down some steps on the other side of Widmouth Head and then climb again to skirt Samson's Bay. As you do so, look over to your left for yet another good view across a field to Combe Martin Bay and the moor beyond. You will find a stile on your right; cross it and follow the path along the top of Samson's Bay, with an attractive wall on your left and a thicket of trees protecting you from the cliff on your right.

Soon the trees give way to bracken, and you get a grand view over the sea to the Welsh coast in the distance. As you round Rillage Point, another lovely vista opens up, along the coast to Ilfracombe. The path climbs inland to the right of some cottages and emerges at a parking area on the A399; turn right and follow a path running alongside the road, separated from it by a wall. After a while it crosses the wall and runs along the grass verge beside the road. You pass a parking and picnic area and the verge gives way to a pavement as you pass Hele Bay.

5. Just beyond the Hele Bay Hotel you part company with the Tarka Trail, which follows the Coast Path to the right. Your route goes left along a footpath just beyond a bus shelter on the other side of the road. This leads you alongside a stream to Hele Mill, an old corn mill and pottery. Go through the mill complex and along a track on the other side to a lane; turn left and follow it as it climbs away from Ilfracombe.

There follows a long and steady climb between high hedges; as you go, look back for a good view across Ilfracombe, and also across the undulating fields to the right. After a little over $\frac{1}{2}$ mile, you come to a junction; go straight on (signposted to Berrynarbor). You now get an excellent view ahead to Little and Great Hangman and the wide expanse of Exmoor, with the sea on your left and the coast of Wales in the distance. The lane starts to descend and after another $\frac{1}{2}$ mile, you enter a small wood and pass under a pretty bridge. The lane swings to the right to descend steeply down the opposite side of the valley from the route you took out of Berrynarbor. At the T-junction turn left and at the next T-junction right to climb a short hill back to the pub and the car park further on.

 ### THE TARKA TRAIL FROM HELE TO DAMAGE HUE (5½ MILES)

Follow the road from the A399 down to the beach. Climb some steps up to the cliff top and follow the Coast Path waymarks to Ilfracombe harbour. Just beyond the slipway go left and then right into Broad Street. At the T-junction turn left into Capstone Crescent. At the end turn right along a path, which eventually emerges onto a road. Turn right and then right again to climb some steps behind the Landmark Theatre to a path. This emerges at another road; turn right into Granville Road. Where the road bears left down a hill, go straight on along a track.

At the end turn right onto a drive and bear left. Follow a path along the cliff and then up a hill to a track. Follow it until it becomes a lane just outside Lee, then follow the lane, turning right to go through the village and up a hill to Damage Hue, where you meet the next walk.

MORTEHOE
The Ship Aground

There are some quite magnificent views along this stretch of the coast. The Tarka Trail continues to follow the route of the South West Coast Path, sweeping down to cross the occasional stream and then climbing steeply out of the valley again, opening up a different panorama each time. This makes it quite hard going at times, but the rewards are breathtaking. The routes to and from the Trail are fairly easy, following lanes and farm paths.

This delightful little inn was originally three 16th century cottages. It has in fact only been a pub since 1980, but it has been beautifully converted. It is full of character, with low beams, a lovely open fireplace, whitewashed walls with the stone exposed in places and tree stumps as tables.

The accommodation comprises three interconnecting sections, the front two of which are bars while the rear comprises a family room with a skittle alley. Both dogs and children are welcome, and the opening hours are 11 am to 3 pm and 6 pm to 11 pm on Monday to Saturday, with the usual more restricted Sunday hours.

There is a good selection of beer on tap, including Cotleigh Tawney, Flowers, Wadworth 6X and Boddingtons, as well as Whitbread Best bitter, Heineken and Stella Artois lager, Blackthorn and Woodpecker cider and Murphy's stout. The food ranges from pasties and burgers to a range of fish, steak and vegetarian offerings. Telephone: 01271 870856.

- **GETTING THERE:** Turn right off the B3343, which runs west from the A361 Barnstaple to Ilfracombe road, and follow the signs to Mortehoe. The pub is in the centre of the village, opposite the church.
- **PARKING:** The pub has no car park, but there is a public car park on the left as you enter the village.
- **LENGTH OF THE WALK:** 5$\frac{1}{4}$ miles. Maps: OS Landranger 180 Barnstaple and Ilfracombe; OS Explorer 139 Bideford, Ilfracombe and Barnstaple (GR 457453).

THE WALK

1. Follow the main road back through the village and take the first turning left (signposted to the lighthouse and Lee). Follow the lane out of the village, and where it ends, go through a gate and continue along the private road that leads to Bull Point lighthouse. It winds between high hedges, with an excellent view ahead across a patchwork of fields to Lee Bay.

2. After about $\frac{1}{2}$ mile, the road turns sharply to the left; at this point you should leave it and go through a gap in the fence on the right and down some steps (signposted to Lee and Bennett's Mouth). You go steeply down, twisting and turning through a small wood, to a stream. At the path junction go right (signposted to Lee), cross a small footbridge and climb rather more gently up the other side of the valley to a gate.

Keep to the fence on the other side, and at the far corner of the field cross a stile and turn right along a track. Go through a gate and turn immediately left across a stile. Keep to the right of the field beyond to another stile. The path now runs between banks and hedges to a lane; go straight on.

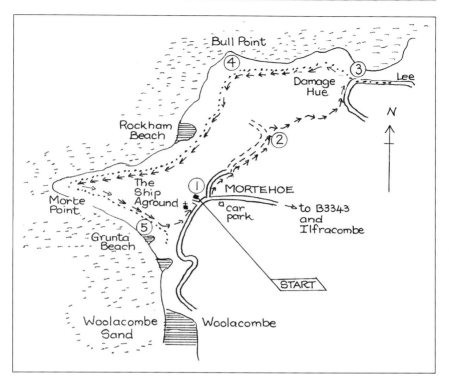

3. After about ¼ mile, just before the lane swings sharply to the right, turn left through a gate and up some steps, following the sign for the Coast Path and the Tarka Trail to Woolacombe. Follow the path up through the field to the cliffs. You can look back here up the valley behind you to the attractive village of Lee.

The clear path leads you down into a couple of valleys and out again, across footbridges and stiles. Some of the hills are steep, but with each climb the view back along the coast becomes more spectacular, so do stop from time to time to catch your breath and admire it.

4. About a mile after joining the Trail, you will pass Bull Point and its lighthouse. Keep to the path along the edge of the cliff, crossing the track to the lighthouse as you go. You round the point and the path continues to climb and descend, still crossing stiles from time to time. You now begin to get some grand views ahead of you to the bracken-covered slopes leading down to the rocks below.

As you approach Morte Point, you will find different paths going off to the left; ignore them and keep to the main path alongside the coastline. Look back for another superb view round Rockham Bay to Bull Point and the lighthouse. As you round Morte Point, a different view greets you – a stunning panorama round Morte Bay, with the long stretch of Woolacombe Sand almost straight ahead and the crags of Baggy Point to the right. Just off Morte Point is the Morte Stone, where Tarka took shelter after being buffeted by the fierce waves on his journey along the coast.

Cross one last stile and just above Grunta Beach you will come to a path junction in front of some houses, with one path going straight up the hill ahead, another veering left and the Coast Path going to the right, below the houses.

5. This is where you leave the Tarka Trail. Take the path that goes left, climbing gently up the hill to a gate leading onto a lane. Turn left and follow the lane back to Mortehoe. You will find the Ship Aground on the left just beyond the church.

🐾 THE TARKA TRAIL FROM GRUNTA BEACH TO SAUNTON (9½ MILES)

The Trail continues to follow the route of the Coast Path along the cliff top to a road, which it then follows to Woolacombe. It passes through a car park and then goes right along a road above the beach. After a while it branches off to the right to Woolacombe Warren.

At the end of the Warren it goes up some steps to a track and then a road, which it follows for about 200 yards before going right onto a track to follow the coastline round Baggy Point. At Croyde Bay it joins a lane, which it follows through the village, and then leaves it again to go right along the edge of the beach. At the end of the sand it climbs up to the cliff top and then follows the coast round before climbing up to a road.

It goes left along the road and then sharp right to run above it to the Saunton Sands Hotel, where it crosses over and makes a brief detour to the beach. From there it follows a track back to the road, which it follows for a few hundred yards to a lane leading off to the right. This is where the next walk joins it.

GEORGEHAM
The Rock Inn
❦

This route follows a pretty, often flower-filled, green lane over a ridge to join the Tarka Trail at Saunton Sands. It then skirts the dunes of Braunton Burrows ('the low, rugged lines of the Burrows' as Williamson describes them), before leaving the Trail and returning to Georgeham via quiet country lanes. There is some climbing involved, but it is not excessive and the reward, as you look out over the surrounding farmland and seashore from the top of the ridge, is out of all proportion to the effort.

Georgeham has a special place in Tarka lore, as it was here that Henry Williamson lived for many years, and this is where he wrote much of *Tarka the Otter*. A brief exploration of the village reveals various reminders of his life, including his home and his grave.

The Rock Inn is a charming 17th century pub, with the low beams typical of the era and a tiled floor. In addition to the main bar, which is decorated with a interesting collection of foreign bank notes, you will find a pleasant garden and a beautiful, airy conservatory filled with plants. Dogs are allowed, as long as they are on leads, and children are welcome in the conservatory and garden but not in the main bar.

The pub is noted for its Rock Inn rolls – 16 inch rolls with a variety of fillings. The menu also includes jacket potatoes and a range of fish, steak and pasta dishes. They pride themselves on using the best fresh produce. There is a wide range of drinks on tap. Two guest beers are offered in addition to a variety of regulars: Ruddles County, Wadworth 6X, Abbot Ale, Theakston Old Peculier, John Smith's, Courage Best, Beck's, Budweiser, Foster's and Carlsberg lagers, Scrumpy Jack cider and Guinness. Opening hours are 11 am to 3 pm and 6 pm to 11 pm on weekdays and all day at weekends. Telephone: 01271 890322.

- **GETTING THERE:** If you are approaching from the south, take the B3231 from Braunton to Croyde and continue into Georgeham. From the north, take the B3343, which runs west from the A361 Barnstaple to Ilfracombe road, and turn off left, following the signs for Georgeham. The Rock Inn is in Rock Hill, which goes east off the main road in the centre of the village, and is signposted.

- **PARKING:** Please ask about leaving your car in the pub car park while you walk as it can become crowded, especially in summer. Otherwise there is parking in some of the side roads in the village (though not in Rock Hill itself).

- **LENGTH OF THE WALK:** 6^3/$_4$ miles. Maps: OS Landranger 180 Barnstaple and Ilfracombe; OS Explorer 139 Bideford, Ilfracombe and Barnstaple (GR 466399).

THE WALK

1. Turn right as you leave the pub and follow Rock Hill down to the main road; turn left. You pass the church on your right; Henry Williamson's grave can still be seen in the churchyard. Follow the road out of the village towards Croyde. Take care along here, as there is no pavement and the road can become quite busy in summer. After about ^{3}/$_4$ mile it takes a sharp turn to the right and you will see a small lane leading off to the left; turn up it.

2. You pass South Hole Farm on your right and shortly after it you will see a public bridleway sign pointing up the bank; follow that. It points you to a track, which takes you past some farm buildings to a gate, where it joins another track. Go straight on, past some more farm buildings, and the track becomes a green lane climbing up the ridge

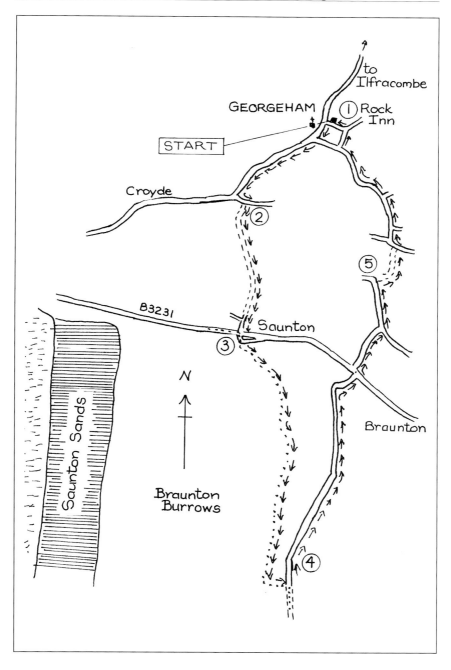

which separates the farmland of Georgeham from the beach and dunes of Saunton Sands and Braunton Burrows. It climbs steadily between high banks filled with flowers in summer, but when you emerge at the top you get a delightful view back across the patchwork of fields to the sea.

At the junction at the top go straight on (signposted to Saunton). You now get a magnificent view ahead of you, across Braunton Burrows to the Taw and Torridge estuary, with the expanse of Saunton Sands on your right. After a while you begin to descend, and you pass a small wood stretching down to the valley on your right. You emerge onto a lane; go straight on, passing the beautiful manor house of Saunton Court as you go. At the next junction, go straight on to the B3231.

🐾 **3.** Cross the road to a lane; this is where you join the Tarka Trail, which still follows the route of the South West Coast Path. When the lane turns sharp left, go straight on through a gate and bear left to follow a path between some mounds to another gate. This takes you onto a sandy path which skirts Saunton Golf Course. Beyond the golf course, you can see the dunes of Braunton Burrows, one of the largest sand dune systems in the country.

Saunton Court

After about $1/2$ mile, the route leaves the main path and goes off to the left, as indicated by the public bridleway sign. After a while it goes through a wooded area and finally leaves the golf course via a gate. Continue through the scrub and bushes on the edge of the Burrows to another gate. You are now in a military firing area, so keep to the path, particularly if there are flags flying to your right. The path emerges onto a broad track; turn left and follow the track to a car park.

4. At the end of the car park turn left into a lane. This is where you leave the Tarka Trail, which goes to the right. The lane goes almost dead straight, with just a couple of kinks, for about $1^1/4$ miles. The area through which it passes is very flat, but there are pretty flowers in the hedgerows in season, and the ridge which rises in the distance ahead of you is a patchwork of fields and farms.

Ignore the turnings to the right and eventually the lane will take a twist to the right and then to the left and emerge at the B3231. Go left and then immediately right (signposted to Lobb) to climb gently to a T-junction; turn left. If you look through the gateways to the left as you go along here, you will get a very good view across Braunton Burrows to the sea.

5. When the lane turns sharply to the left in a farm, turn right into a green lane. It climbs quite steeply and swings to the left, still climbing. After about $1/4$ mile it emerges onto a lane; turn left and at the junction go straight on, following the main lane (signposted to Darracott and Georgeham). You are now at the top of the ridge and can once again stop to enjoy the extensive view ahead across the rich fields.

At the next junction, go straight on (signposted to Darracott and Georgeham again). The lane now begins to descend and you come to another junction; go straight on again (signposted to Georgeham). It winds its way into Georgeham, and at the next junction you should turn right into Longland Lane. At the end, where Longland Lane meets Rock Hill, turn left to return to the pub.

WALK 20

BRAUNTON
The George Hotel
❧❦❧

This undemanding ramble is full of interest, taking in one of the few examples of medieval open-field cultivation left in England, a system of sand dunes that is home to over 400 species of flowering plant and a once-bustling commercial quay, now used only by pleasure craft. It was here that Tarka and his mate suffered the rigours of the 'Great Winter'. This area is completely flat, and the walking is consequently very easy throughout the route.

Built in the 1920s, the George still retains something of the atmosphere of the period. There is an almost genteel charm about it, and the understated decor and comfortable furnishings are reminiscent of that era.

There are two main rooms: a spacious bar and an attractive tearoom/restaurant. The carpeted bar has a large bay window at one end, which makes it pleasantly light and airy, while the restaurant is a more intimate room, with leaded windows and a bare wooden floor covered in rugs. The latter serves two functions: it is a tearoom by day, serving light lunches, coffees and teas, and a restaurant by night with a full menu. There is a traditional roast lunch on Sundays. Food is also available in the bar, and ranges from sandwiches to traditional bar meals such as scampi and ham and eggs, using only local produce wherever possible. Children are only allowed in the bar if they are eating there, but they are welcome in the tearoom. Dogs are allowed in the bar.

Wadworth 6X, Tetley, Boddingtons and Flowers are the draught beers, as well as Stella Artois, Heineken and Heineken Export lagers, Caffrey's ale, Dry Blackthorn cider, Guinness and Murphy's stout. Bar hours are 11 am to 11 pm on Mondays to Saturdays and 12 noon to 10.30 pm on Sundays (although the tearoom is open from 8 am every day), and accommodation is available for those wanting to spend more time exploring this fascinating and beautiful area. Telephone: 01271 812029.

- **GETTING THERE:** The A361 Barnstaple to Ilfracombe road runs straight through Braunton, and the George Hotel is on the main road (Exeter Road) in the centre of the village.
- **PARKING:** The hotel car park is on the opposite side of Exeter Road from the hotel itself, and the landlord has no objection to customers leaving their cars there while they walk, provided they ask first. Alternatively, there is a free public car park a little to the north of the hotel on the road to Croyde.
- **LENGTH OF THE WALK:** $6^3/_4$ miles. Maps: OS Landranger 180 Barnstaple and Ilfracombe; OS Explorer 139 Bideford, Ilfracombe and Barnstaple (GR 488365).

THE WALK

1. As you leave the George, turn left and then immediately left again into South Street. After about 150 yards, turn right into Sings Lane, and at the end go left and almost immediately right. Cross a small bridge and turn left along a surfaced path on the other side. After a few yards turn right along another surfaced path between houses. This emerges onto a road; turn left.

2. About 50 yards along this road, turn right onto a track between hedges. It emerges into an enormous, unfenced, cultivated area. This is Braunton Great Field, a remnant of the system of open-field cultivation

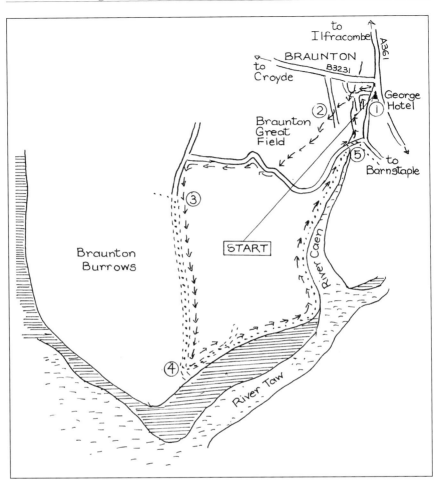

which was used across much of lowland England during the Middle Ages. At that time about 100 farmers would have worked the area, each cultivating a strip of land and co-operating with each other to agree what crops should be planted; now there are just five.

The track curves to the left and you will come to a junction; turn right, and follow this new track in an almost straight line to the end of the field. As you go, you will be able to see the dunes of Braunton Burrows half right. Cross a stile into a lane and turn right. The lane winds to the left and to the right, and then goes dead straight for 700 yards to a T-junction; turn left and continue for ¼ mile.

🐾 **3.** You come to a car park on your right and the lane becomes a rough track. This is where you join the Tarka Trail, which comes in from the right through the car park. Continue along the track, passing a gate as you go. The track skirts Braunton Burrows, a national nature reserve comprising over 4 square miles of sand dunes running inland from the 4-mile beach of Saunton Sands. If you want to explore them there are plenty of paths going off to the right, but this is a military training area so you should not venture off the track if there are red flags flying.

You pass another gate and soon you will be able to see Appledore across the estuary ahead of you. After passing a third gate you will come to a junction, with a large parking area ahead and a boardwalk leading to the beach on your right.

4. Turn left here to follow another sandy track, passing more parking areas as you go. You will see a white house ahead of you on the right; turn right in front of it, following the Coast Path sign and the Tarka Trail waymark. Just before this new track comes out at the water's edge, turn left up some steps onto a dyke, following the Coast Path waymark.

Low tide on the River Caen

The dyke runs as straight as a die for $3/4$ mile, with the marshes and farmland of Horsey Island on the left and the broad River Taw on the right. It then curves inland to follow the River Caen. You cross a stone stile and then a wooden one, and the dyke runs alongside a lane. Cross two walls via stone steps and you will come to a car park. This is the site of Velator Quay, once used for the shipment of local produce but made redundant by the coming of the railway and now used only by pleasure craft.

Go through the car park and along the path on the other side. When you come to a weir turn left and go up a set of steps and then down another set to reach a road; turn right, following the Coast Path sign.

5. Just before the road meets another at a T-junction, go left along a surfaced path; this is where you leave the Tarka Trail, which goes to the right. The path runs between the river on the left and some houses on the right, and finally emerges onto a road. Turn left and at the end follow it round to the right. You are now back in Sings Lane; at the T-junction at the end, turn left into South Street to return to the George Hotel.

🐾 THE TARKA TRAIL FROM BRAUNTON TO BARNSTAPLE ($5^{1}/_{2}$ MILES)

The route turns right alongside the road and follows the disused railway line for about $4^{1}/_{2}$ miles. On the outskirts of Barnstaple it turns away from the river and follows a track to a lane. At the end of the lane it goes right and after 100 yards right again. At the main road at the end it goes right across Rolle Bridge and then immediately right again. Just beyond the old railway station it turns right again to rejoin the river. It crosses the river via the Long Bridge and at the roundabout on the other side bears left to finish at Barnstaple Station.